FUN BIBLE
Picture
Games
FOR
KIDS

Published by Barbour Publishing, Inc., P.O. Box 719, Uhrichsville, Ohio 44683
www.barbourbooks.com

Our mission is to publish and distribute inspirational products offering exceptional value and biblical encouragement to the masses.

 Member of the
Evangelical Christian
Publishers Association

Printed in the United States of America.
Offset Paperback Mfrs., Inc., Dallas, PA; Print Code D10002502; September 2010

FUN BIBLE Picture Games FOR KIDS

BARBOUR
PUBLISHING

ABRAHAM

WHO *WAS* ABRAHAM? WHY WAS THIS MAN SO IMPORTANT?

ABRAHAM WAS CALLED RIGHTEOUS. WHY? WAS HE A GOOD PERSON? DID HE ALWAYS DO WHAT WAS RIGHT? DID HE EVER DO SOMETHING WRONG WHEN HE WAS AFRAID? DID HE ALWAYS TRUST GOD? DID HE EVER TELL A LIE? DID HE EVER ASK ANOTHER TO TELL A LIE FOR HIM? WAS ABRAHAM CONSIDERED RIGHTEOUS BY HOW HE LIVED AND ACTED, OR BECAUSE HE BELIEVED GOD AND HIS PROMISES?

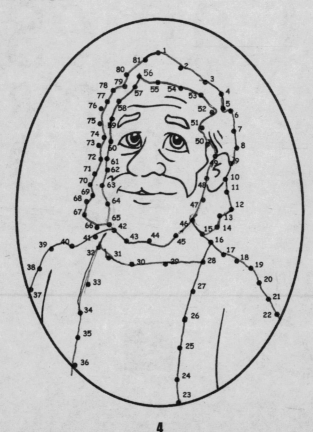

FAMiLY MATTERS

"TERAH TOOK HIS SON ABRAM, HIS GRANDSON LOT SON OF HARAN, AND HIS DAUGHTER-IN-LAW SARAI, THE WIFE OF HIS SON ABRAM, AND TOGETHER THEY SET OUT FROM UR OF THE CHALDEANS TO GO TO CANAAN. BUT WHEN THEY CAME TO HARAN, THEY SETTLED THERE."

GENESIS 11:31

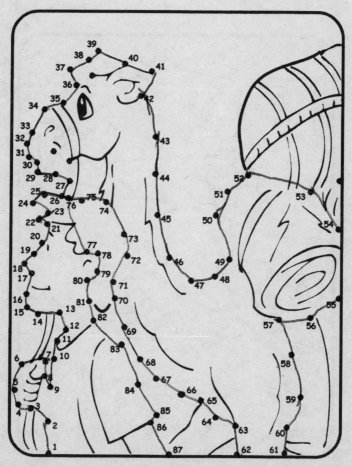

TIME TO MOVE OUT

HAVE YOU EVER WONDERED HOW GOD SPOKE TO ABRAM?

"THE LORD HAD SAID TO ABRAM, 'LEAVE YOUR COUNTRY, YOUR PEOPLE AND YOUR FATHER'S HOUSEHOLD AND GO TO THE LAND I WILL SHOW YOU.'"

GENESIS 12:1

I WILL BLESS YOU

WHY DO YOU THINK GOD CHOSE TO MAKE
ABRAM INTO A GREAT NATION?

God made Abram a great nation. I think because his life was so full of sins he needed

"'I WILL MAKE YOU INTO A GREAT

NATION AND I WILL BLESS YOU; *joy &*

I WILL MAKE YOUR NAME GREAT, *happiness!*

AND YOU WILL BE A BLESSING.'"

GENESIS 12:2

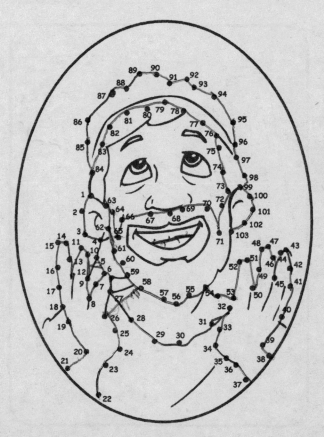

MORE BLESSINGS

WHY WILL ALL PEOPLE ON EARTH BE BLESSED
THROUGH ABRAM?

" 'I WILL BLESS THOSE WHO BLESS YOU,
AND WHOEVER CURSES YOU I WILL
CURSE; AND ALL PEOPLES ON EARTH
WILL BE BLESSED THROUGH YOU.' "

GENESIS 12:3

ON THE ROAD AGAIN

DO YOU EVER WONDER WHAT WAS GOING THROUGH ABRAM'S MIND WHEN GOD ASKED HIM TO MOVE AGAIN? HAVE YOU EVER HAD TO MOVE AGAIN WHEN YOU WERE JUST GETTING SETTLED IN? HOW DID IT MAKE *YOU* FEEL?

> "SO ABRAM LEFT, AS THE LORD HAD TOLD HIM; AND LOT WENT WITH HIM. ABRAM WAS SEVENTY-FIVE YEARS OLD WHEN HE SET OUT FROM HARAN."
>
> GENESIS 12:4

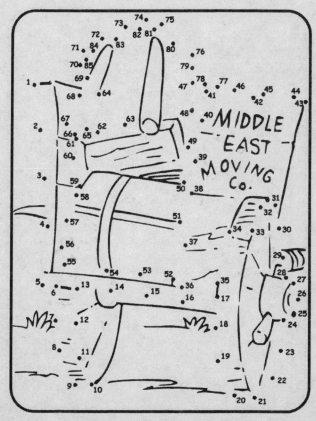

I'M SO HUNGRY!

WHAT DOES IT MEAN WHEN SOMEONE SAYS THERE IS A FAMINE IN THE LAND?

"NOW THERE WAS A FAMINE IN THE LAND, AND ABRAM WENT DOWN TO EGYPT TO LIVE THERE FOR A WHILE BECAUSE THE FAMINE WAS SEVERE."

GENESIS 12:10

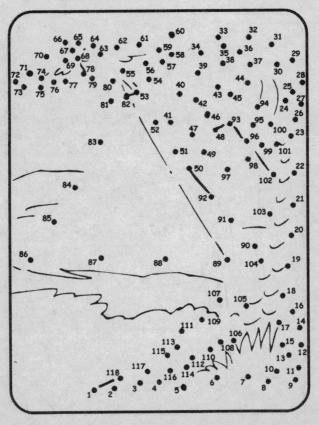

RIGHT OR WRONG

"AS HE WAS ABOUT TO ENTER EGYPT, HE SAID TO HIS WIFE SARAI, 'I KNOW WHAT A BEAUTIFUL WOMAN YOU ARE. WHEN THE EGYPTIANS SEE YOU, THEY WILL SAY, "THIS IS HIS WIFE." THEN THEY WILL KILL ME BUT WILL LET YOU LIVE. SAY YOU ARE MY SISTER, SO THAT I WILL BE TREATED WELL FOR YOUR SAKE AND MY LIFE WILL BE SPARED BECAUSE OF YOU.'"

GENESIS 12:11–13

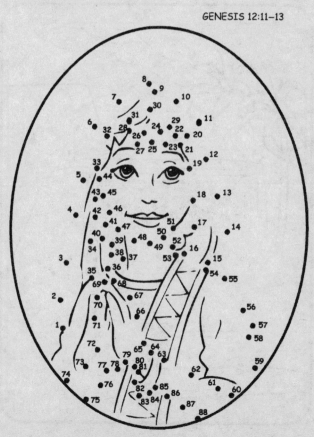

SAY WHAT?

HAVE YOU EVER ASKED SOMEONE ELSE TO LIE FOR YOU? HOW DOES THIS AFFECT THE OTHER PERSON?

"WHEN ABRAM CAME TO EGYPT, THE EGYPTIANS SAW THAT SHE WAS A VERY BEAUTIFUL WOMAN. AND WHEN PHARAOH'S OFFICIALS SAW HER, THEY PRAISED HER TO PHARAOH, AND SHE WAS TAKEN INTO HIS PALACE."

GENESIS 12:14–15

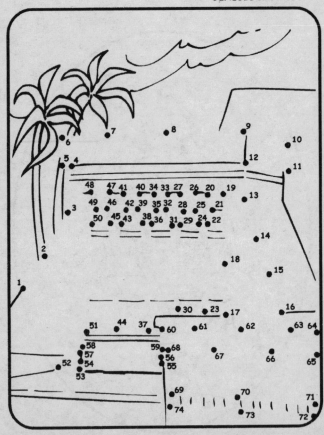

IT LOOKS PROFITABLE

IT LOOKS LIKE ABRAM PROFITED BY LYING ABOUT WHO SARAI WAS. BUT... *DOES* HE?

> "HE TREATED ABRAM WELL FOR HER SAKE, AND ABRAM ACQUIRED SHEEP AND CATTLE, MALE AND FEMALE DONKEYS, MENSERVANTS AND MAIDSERVANTS, AND CAMELS."

GENESIS 12:16

YOU CAN'T LIE TO GOD

YOU MAY BE ABLE TO LIE TO PEOPLE BUT YOU CAN'T LIE TO GOD.

"BUT THE LORD INFLICTED SERIOUS DISEASES ON PHARAOH AND HIS HOUSEHOLD BECAUSE OF ABRAM'S WIFE SARAI."

GENESIS 12:17

THE TRUTH COMES OUT

"SO PHARAOH SUMMONED ABRAM. 'WHAT HAVE YOU DONE TO ME?' HE SAID. 'WHY DIDN'T YOU TELL ME SHE WAS YOUR WIFE? WHY DID YOU SAY, "SHE IS MY SISTER," SO THAT I TOOK HER TO BE MY WIFE? NOW THEN, HERE IS YOUR WIFE. TAKE HER AND GO!'"

GENESIS 12:18–19

PACKING AGAIN

ABRAM ONCE AGAIN PACKED UP HIS FAMILY AND HOUSEHOLD AND MOVED ON.

"SO ABRAM WENT UP FROM EGYPT TO THE NEGEV, WITH HIS WIFE AND EVERYTHING HE HAD, AND LOT WENT WITH HIM. ABRAM HAD BECOME VERY WEALTHY IN LIVESTOCK AND IN SILVER AND GOLD."

GENESIS 13:1–2

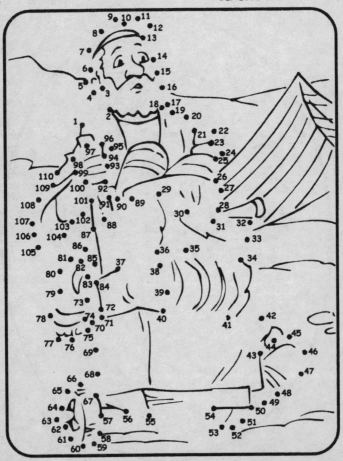

SECOND CHANCES

GOD CONTINUED TO SPEAK WITH ABRAM AND PROMISED HIM GREAT THINGS EVEN AFTER HE DID WHAT WAS WRONG. ARE THERE SECOND CHANCES WITH GOD?

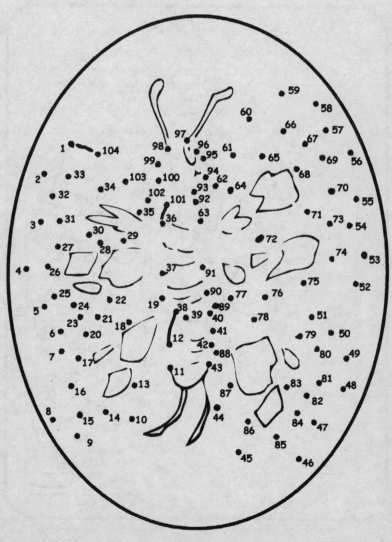

DUST OF THE EARTH

GOD SOMETIMES GIVES WHAT APPEAR TO BE *IMPOSSIBLE* PROMISES. BUT...ALL THINGS ARE POSSIBLE WITH GOD.

PACKING YET AGAIN

WHY DID ABRAM BUILD AN ALTAR TO THE LORD? IS THIS ABRAM'S WAY OF REMEMBERING WHAT GOD HAS DONE FOR HIM AND HIS PROMISES TO HIM?

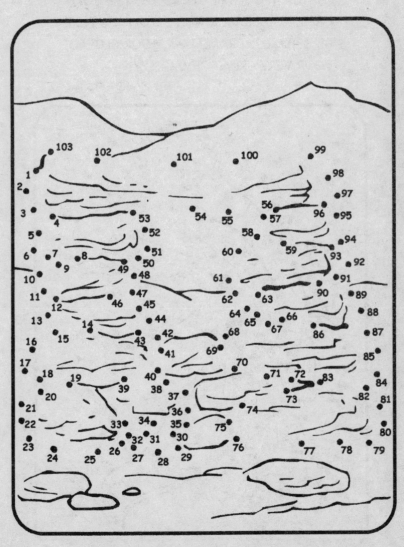

DO NOT BE AFRAID

HAVE YOU EVER WONDERED WHAT A *VISION* IS? IS IT A DREAM OR IS IT LIKE WATCHING A MOVIE?

"AFTER THIS, THE WORD OF THE LORD CAME TO ABRAM IN A VISION: 'DO NOT BE AFRAID, ABRAM. I AM YOUR SHIELD, YOUR VERY GREAT REWARD.'"

GENESIS 15:1

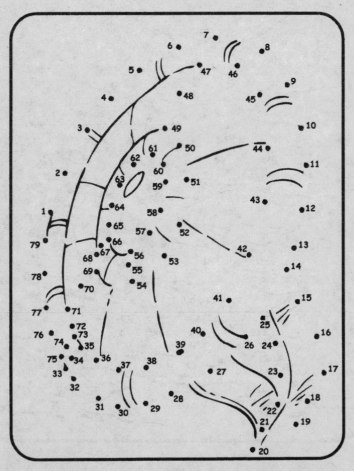

GOD UNDERSTANDS

"THEN THE WORD OF THE LORD CAME TO HIM: 'THIS MAN WILL NOT BE YOUR HEIR, BUT A SON COMING FROM YOUR OWN BODY WILL BE YOUR HEIR.' HE TOOK HIM OUTSIDE AND SAID, 'LOOK UP AT THE HEAVENS AND COUNT THE STARS—IF INDEED YOU CAN COUNT THEM.' THEN HE SAID TO HIM, 'SO SHALL YOUR OFFSPRING BE.'"

GENESIS 15:4–5

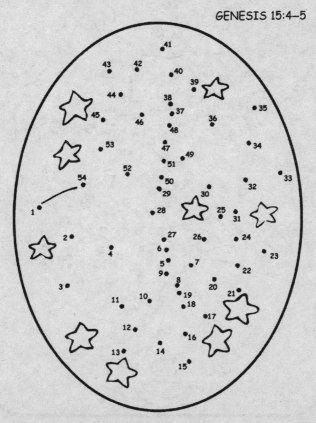

I BELIEVE YOU, LORD

WHAT DOES IT MEAN TO BELIEVE GOD? DO YOU HAVE A HARD TIME TAKING GOD AT HIS WORD?

"ABRAM BELIEVED THE LORD, AND HE CREDITED IT TO HIM AS RIGHTEOUSNESS."

GENESIS 15:6

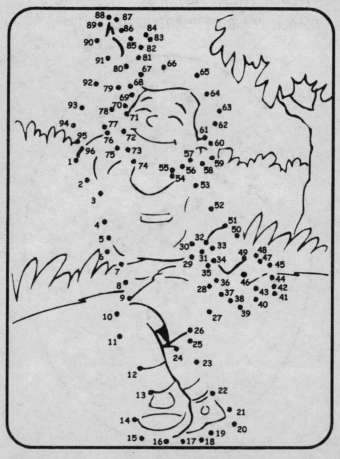

A COVENANT

"ON THAT DAY THE LORD MADE A COVENANT WITH ABRAM AND SAID, 'TO YOUR DESCENDANTS I GIVE THIS LAND, FROM THE RIVER OF EGYPT TO THE GREAT RIVER, THE EUPHRATES—THE LAND OF THE KENITES, KENIZZITES, KADMONITES, HITTITES, PERIZZITES, REPHAITES, AMORITES, CANAANITES, GIRGASHITES AND JEBUSITES.'"

GENESIS 15:18–21

SARAI

"NOW SARAI, ABRAM'S WIFE, HAD BORNE HIM NO CHILDREN. BUT SHE HAD AN EGYPTIAN MAIDSERVANT NAMED HAGAR; SO SHE SAID TO ABRAM, 'THE LORD HAS KEPT ME FROM HAVING CHILDREN. GO, SLEEP WITH MY MAIDSERVANT; PERHAPS I CAN BUILD A FAMILY THROUGH HER.' ABRAM AGREED TO WHAT SARAI SAID."

GENESIS 16:1–2

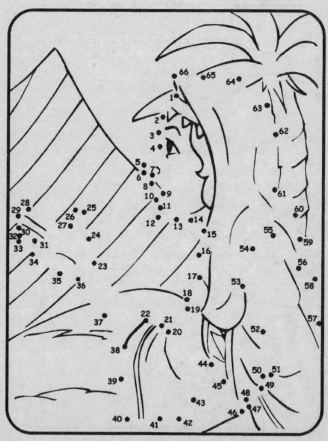

BLAMING OTHERS

"WHEN SHE KNEW SHE WAS PREGNANT, SHE BEGAN TO DESPISE HER MISTRESS. THEN SARAI SAID TO ABRAM, 'YOU ARE RESPONSIBLE FOR THE WRONG I AM SUFFERING. I PUT MY SERVANT IN YOUR ARMS, AND NOW THAT SHE KNOWS SHE IS PREGNANT, SHE DESPISES ME. MAY THE LORD JUDGE BETWEEN YOU AND ME.'"

GENESIS 16:4–5

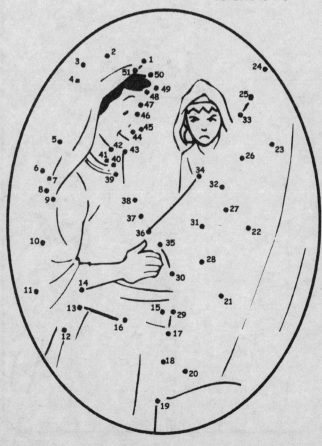

WALK BEFORE ME

"WHEN ABRAM WAS NINETY-NINE YEARS OLD, THE LORD APPEARED TO HIM AND SAID, 'I AM GOD ALMIGHTY; WALK BEFORE ME AND BE BLAMELESS. I WILL CONFIRM MY COVENANT BETWEEN ME AND YOU AND WILL GREATLY INCREASE YOUR NUMBERS.'"

GENESIS 17:1–2

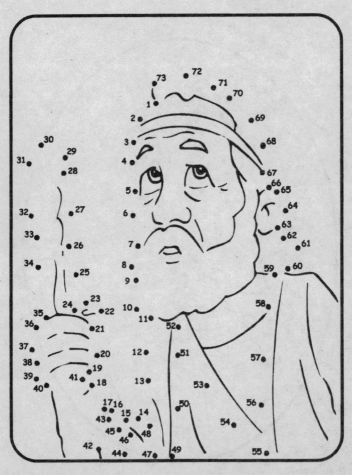

FATHER OF MANY

"ABRAM FELL FACEDOWN, AND GOD SAID TO HIM, 'AS FOR ME, THIS IS MY COVENANT WITH YOU: YOU WILL BE THE FATHER OF MANY NATIONS. NO LONGER WILL YOU BE CALLED ABRAM; YOUR NAME WILL BE ABRAHAM, FOR I HAVE MADE YOU A FATHER OF MANY NATIONS.'"

GENESIS 17:3–5

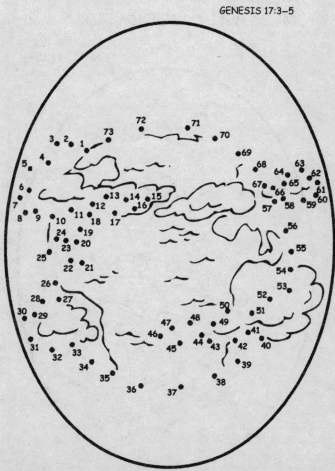

NEW NAMES

"GOD ALSO SAID TO ABRAHAM, 'AS FOR SARAI YOUR WIFE, YOU ARE NO LONGER TO CALL HER SARAI; HER NAME WILL BE SARAH. I WILL BLESS HER AND WILL SURELY GIVE YOU A SON BY HER. I WILL BLESS HER SO THAT SHE WILL BE THE MOTHER OF NATIONS; KINGS OF PEOPLES WILL COME FROM HER.'"

GENESIS 17:15–16

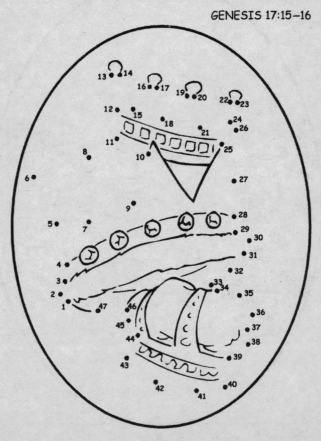

AT MY AGE?

"ABRAHAM FELL FACEDOWN; HE LAUGHED AND SAID TO HIMSELF, 'WILL A SON BE BORN TO A MAN A HUNDRED YEARS OLD? WILL SARAH BEAR A CHILD AT THE AGE OF NINETY?' AND ABRAHAM SAID TO GOD, 'IF ONLY ISHMAEL MIGHT LIVE UNDER YOUR BLESSING!'"

GENESIS 17:17–18

ISAAC

GOD NOT ONLY PROMISED ABRAHAM A SON BUT NAMED HIS SON FOR HIM. I WONDER WHAT THE NAME ISAAC MEANS?

"THEN GOD SAID, 'YES, BUT YOUR WIFE SARAH WILL BEAR YOU A SON, AND YOU WILL CALL HIM ISAAC. I WILL ESTABLISH MY COVENANT WITH HIM AS AN EVERLASTING COVENANT FOR HIS DESCENDANTS AFTER HIM.'"

GENESIS 17:19

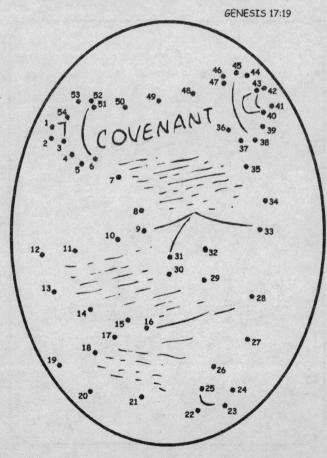

TREES OF MAMRE

"THE LORD APPEARED TO ABRAHAM NEAR THE GREAT TREES OF MAMRE WHILE HE WAS SITTING AT THE ENTRANCE TO HIS TENT IN THE HEAT OF THE DAY. ABRAHAM LOOKED UP AND SAW THREE MEN STANDING NEARBY. WHEN HE SAW THEM, HE HURRIED FROM THE ENTRANCE OF HIS TENT TO MEET THEM AND BOWED LOW TO THE GROUND."

GENESIS 18:1–2

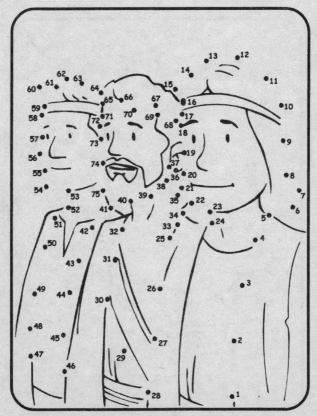

FOUND FAVOR

"HE SAID, 'IF I HAVE FOUND FAVOR IN YOUR EYES, MY LORD, DO NOT PASS YOUR SERVANT BY. LET A LITTLE WATER BE BROUGHT, AND THEN YOU MAY ALL WASH YOUR FEET AND REST UNDER THIS TREE. LET ME GET YOU SOMETHING TO EAT, SO YOU CAN BE REFRESHED AND THEN GO ON YOUR WAY—NOW THAT YOU HAVE COME TO YOUR SERVANT.'

"'VERY WELL,' THEY ANSWERED, 'DO AS YOU SAY.'"

GENESIS 18:3–5

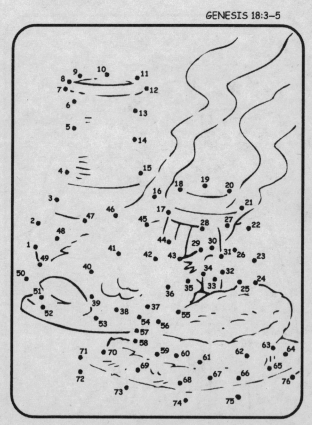

NeXt YeAR

GOD DOESN'T JUST TELL ABRAHAM THAT HE IS TO HAVE A SON, BUT *WHEN* HE WILL BE BORN.

"THEN THE LORD SAID, 'I WILL SURELY RETURN TO YOU ABOUT THIS TIME NEXT YEAR, AND SARAH YOUR WIFE WILL HAVE A SON.'"

GENESIS 18:10

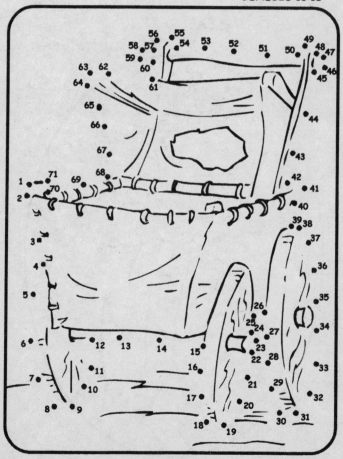

WHEN I'M TIRED

"NOW SARAH WAS LISTENING AT THE ENTRANCE TO THE TENT, WHICH WAS BEHIND HIM. ABRAHAM AND SARAH WERE ALREADY OLD AND WELL ADVANCED IN YEARS, AND SARAH WAS PAST THE AGE OF CHILDBEARING. SO SARAH LAUGHED TO HERSELF AS SHE THOUGHT, 'AFTER I AM WORN OUT AND MY MASTER IS OLD, WILL I NOW HAVE THIS PLEASURE?'"

GENESIS 18:10–12

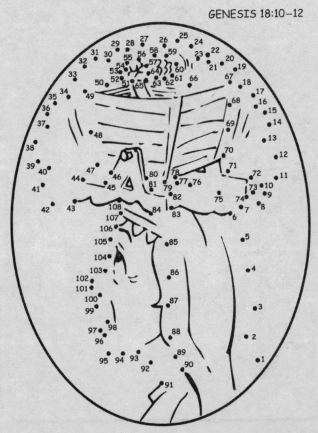

ANYTHING IS POSSIBLE

"THEN THE LORD SAID TO ABRAHAM, 'WHY DID SARAH LAUGH AND SAY, "WILL I REALLY HAVE A CHILD, NOW THAT I AM OLD?" IS ANYTHING TOO HARD FOR THE LORD? I WILL RETURN TO YOU AT THE APPOINTED TIME NEXT YEAR AND SARAH WILL HAVE A SON.'"

GENESIS 18:13–14

NOT AGAIN

"NOW ABRAHAM MOVED ON FROM THERE INTO THE REGION OF THE NEGEV AND LIVED BETWEEN KADESH AND SHUR. FOR A WHILE HE STAYED IN GERAR, AND THERE ABRAHAM SAID OF HIS WIFE SARAH, 'SHE IS MY SISTER.' THEN ABIMELECH KING OF GERAR SENT FOR SARAH AND TOOK HER."

GENESIS 20:1–2

SHE'S MARRIED

HOW DO YOU THINK THIS LIE AFFECTED ABIMELECH'S VIEW OF ABRAHAM?

"BUT GOD CAME TO ABIMELECH IN A DREAM ONE NIGHT AND SAID TO HIM, 'YOU ARE AS GOOD AS DEAD BECAUSE OF THE WOMAN YOU HAVE TAKEN; SHE IS A MARRIED WOMAN.'"

GENESIS 20:3

WHY?

"THEN ABIMELECH CALLED ABRAHAM IN AND SAID, 'WHAT HAVE YOU DONE TO US? HOW HAVE I WRONGED YOU THAT YOU HAVE BROUGHT SUCH GREAT GUILT UPON ME AND MY KINGDOM? YOU HAVE DONE THINGS TO ME THAT SHOULD NOT BE DONE.' AND ABIMELECH ASKED ABRAHAM, 'WHAT WAS YOUR REASON FOR DOING THIS?'"

GENESIS 20:9–10

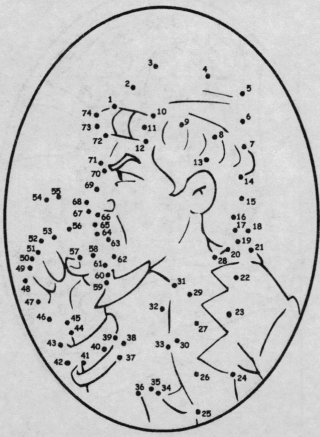

HALF-TRUTHS

"ABRAHAM REPLIED, 'I SAID TO MYSELF, "THERE IS SURELY NO FEAR OF GOD IN THIS PLACE, AND THEY WILL KILL ME BECAUSE OF MY WIFE." BESIDES, SHE REALLY IS MY SISTER, THE DAUGHTER OF MY FATHER THOUGH NOT OF MY MOTHER; AND SHE BECAME MY WIFE. AND WHEN GOD HAD ME WANDER FROM MY FATHER'S HOUSEHOLD, I SAID TO HER, "THIS IS HOW YOU CAN SHOW YOUR LOVE TO ME: EVERYWHERE WE GO, SAY OF ME, "HE IS MY BROTHER."'"

GENESIS 20:11–13

NOT GUILTY

WHAT ABRAHAM ASKED SARAH TO DO WAS WRONG, AND ABIMELECH DECLARED HER INNOCENT.

"TO SARAH HE SAID, 'I AM GIVING YOUR BROTHER A THOUSAND SHEKELS OF SILVER. THIS IS TO COVER THE OFFENSE AGAINST YOU BEFORE ALL WHO ARE WITH YOU; YOU ARE COMPLETELY VINDICATED.'"

GENESIS 20:16

HEALED

WHY DO YOU THINK GOD CLOSED UP EVERY
WOMB IN ABIMELECH'S HOUSEHOLD?

"THEN ABRAHAM PRAYED TO GOD, AND
GOD HEALED ABIMELECH, HIS WIFE
AND HIS SLAVE GIRLS SO THEY COULD
HAVE CHILDREN AGAIN, FOR THE LORD
HAD CLOSED UP EVERY WOMB IN
ABIMELECH'S HOUSEHOLD BECAUSE OF
ABRAHAM'S WIFE SARAH."

GENESIS 20:17–18

GOD'S FAITHULNESS

"NOW THE LORD WAS GRACIOUS TO SARAH AS HE HAD SAID, AND THE LORD DID FOR SARAH WHAT HE HAD PROMISED. SARAH BECAME PREGNANT AND BORE A SON TO ABRAHAM IN HIS OLD AGE, AT THE VERY TIME GOD HAD PROMISED HIM."

GENESIS 21:1–2

ISAAC

"ABRAHAM GAVE THE NAME ISAAC TO THE SON SARAH BORE HIM. WHEN HIS SON ISAAC WAS EIGHT DAYS OLD, ABRAHAM CIRCUMCISED HIM, AS GOD COMMANDED HIM. ABRAHAM WAS A HUNDRED YEARS OLD WHEN HIS SON ISAAC WAS BORN TO HIM."

GENESIS 21:3–5

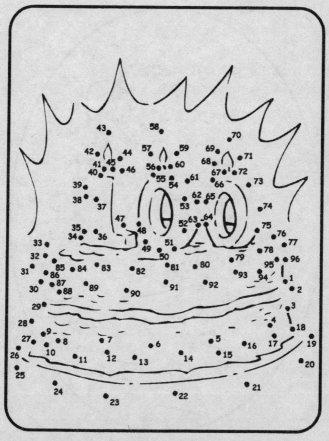

LAUGHTER

"SARAH SAID, 'GOD HAS BROUGHT ME LAUGHTER, AND EVERYONE WHO HEARS ABOUT THIS WILL LAUGH WITH ME.' AND SHE ADDED, 'WHO WOULD HAVE SAID TO ABRAHAM THAT SARAH WOULD NURSE CHILDREN? YET I HAVE BORNE HIM A SON IN HIS OLD AGE.'"

GENESIS 21:6–7

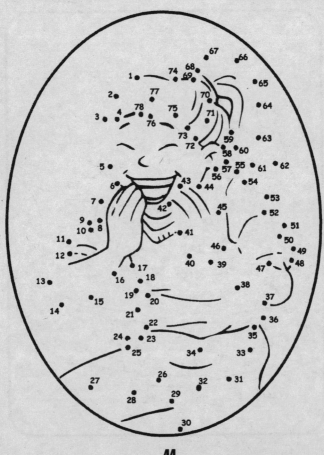

JEALOUSY

"BUT SARAH SAW THAT THE SON
WHOM HAGAR THE EGYPTIAN HAD
BORNE TO ABRAHAM WAS MOCKING,
AND SHE SAID TO ABRAHAM, 'GET RID
OF THAT SLAVE WOMAN AND HER SON,
FOR THAT SLAVE WOMAN'S SON WILL
NEVER SHARE IN THE INHERITANCE
WITH MY SON ISAAC.'"

GENESIS 21:9–10

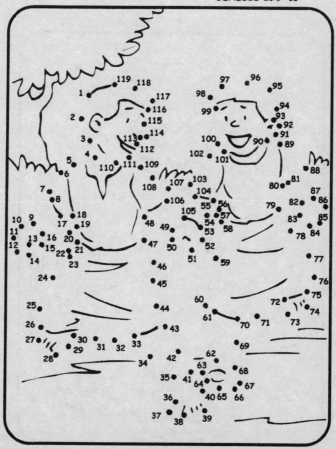

TROUBLED

"THE MATTER DISTRESSED ABRAHAM GREATLY BECAUSE IT CONCERNED HIS SON. BUT GOD SAID TO HIM, 'DO NOT BE SO DISTRESSED ABOUT THE BOY AND YOUR MAIDSERVANT. LISTEN TO WHATEVER SARAH TELLS YOU, BECAUSE IT IS THROUGH ISAAC THAT YOUR OFFSPRING WILL BE RECKONED. I WILL MAKE THE SON OF THE MAIDSERVANT INTO A NATION ALSO, BECAUSE HE IS YOUR OFFSPRING.'"

GENESIS 21:11–13

HAGAR LEAVES

"EARLY THE NEXT MORNING ABRAHAM TOOK SOME FOOD AND A SKIN OF WATER AND GAVE THEM TO HAGAR. HE SET THEM ON HER SHOULDERS AND THEN SENT HER OFF WITH THE BOY. SHE WENT ON HER WAY AND WANDERED IN THE DESERT OF BEERSHEBA."

GENESIS 21:14

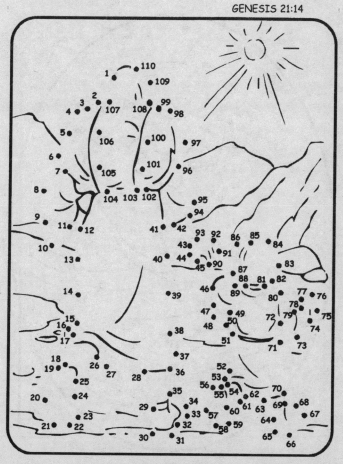

SHE CRIED

"WHEN THE WATER IN THE SKIN WAS GONE, SHE PUT THE BOY UNDER ONE OF THE BUSHES. THEN SHE WENT OFF AND SAT DOWN NEARBY, ABOUT A BOW-SHOT AWAY, FOR SHE THOUGHT, 'I CANNOT WATCH THE BOY DIE.' AND AS SHE SAT THERE NEARBY, SHE BEGAN TO SOB."

GENESIS 21:15–16

FEAR NOT

"GOD HEARD THE BOY CRYING, AND THE ANGEL OF GOD CALLED TO HAGAR FROM HEAVEN AND SAID TO HER, 'WHAT IS THE MATTER, HAGAR? DO NOT BE AFRAID; GOD HAS HEARD THE BOY CRYING AS HE LIES THERE. LIFT THE BOY UP AND TAKE HIM BY THE HAND, FOR I WILL MAKE HIM INTO A GREAT NATION.'"

GENESIS 21:17–18

GOD PROVIDED

"THEN GOD OPENED HER EYES AND SHE SAW A WELL OF WATER. SO SHE WENT AND FILLED THE SKIN WITH WATER AND GAVE THE BOY A DRINK."

GENESIS 21:19

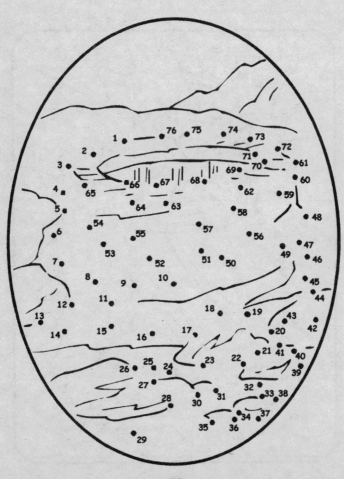

EXCUSE ME, LORD?

"THEN GOD SAID, 'TAKE YOUR SON, YOUR ONLY SON, ISAAC, WHOM YOU LOVE, AND GO TO THE REGION OF MORIAH. SACRIFICE HIM THERE AS A BURNT OFFERING ON ONE OF THE MOUNTAINS I WILL TELL YOU ABOUT.'"

GENESIS 22:2

ALL RIGHT, LORD

"EARLY THE NEXT MORNING ABRAHAM GOT UP AND SADDLED HIS DONKEY. HE TOOK WITH HIM TWO OF HIS SERVANTS AND HIS SON ISAAC. WHEN HE HAD CUT ENOUGH WOOD FOR THE BURNT OFFERING, HE SET OUT FOR THE PLACE GOD HAD TOLD HIM ABOUT."

GENESIS 22:3

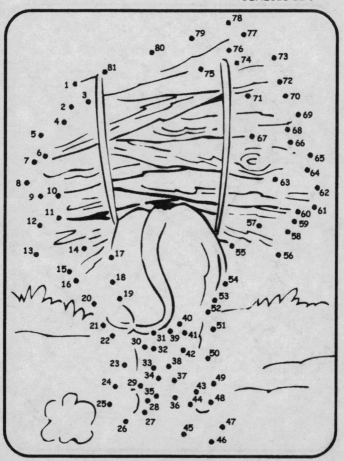

WE WILL COME BACK

"ON THE THIRD DAY ABRAHAM LOOKED UP AND SAW THE PLACE IN THE DISTANCE. HE SAID TO HIS SERVANTS, 'STAY HERE WITH THE DONKEY WHILE I AND THE BOY GO OVER THERE. WE WILL WORSHIP AND THEN WE WILL COME BACK TO YOU.'"

GENESIS 22:4–5

FOLLOWING THROUGH

ABRAHAM WAS DOING AS GOD ASKED, IN SPITE OF WHAT HE MAY HAVE BEEN FEELING.

"ABRAHAM TOOK THE WOOD FOR THE BURNT OFFERING AND PLACED IT ON HIS SON ISAAC, AND HE HIMSELF CARRIED THE FIRE AND THE KNIFE."

GENESIS 22:6

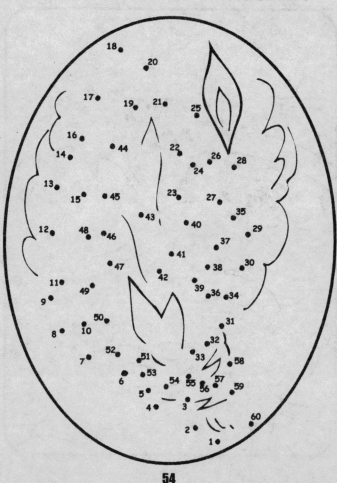

WHAT'S UP, DAD?

"AS THE TWO OF THEM WENT ON TOGETHER, ISAAC SPOKE UP AND SAID TO HIS FATHER ABRAHAM, 'FATHER?'

" 'YES, MY SON?' ABRAHAM REPLIED.

" 'THE FIRE AND WOOD ARE HERE; ISACC SAID, 'BUT WHERE IS THE LAMB FOR THE BURNT OFFERING?' "

GENESIS 22:6-7

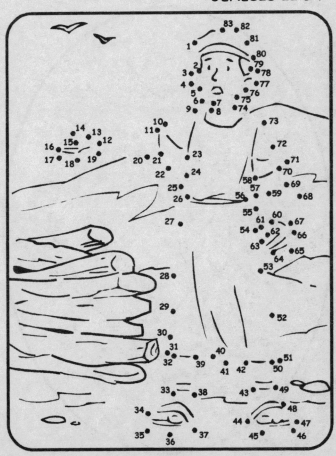

GOD IS IN CONTROL

ABRAHAM TOLD HIS SON ISAAC THAT GOD WOULD PROVIDE THE LAMB.

"ABRAHAM ANSWERED, 'GOD HIMSELF WILL PROVIDE THE LAMB FOR THE BURNT OFFERING, MY SON.' AND THE TWO OF THEM WENT ON TOGETHER."

GENESIS 22:8

ALL THE WAY

"WHEN THEY REACHED THE PLACE GOD
HAD TOLD HIM ABOUT, ABRAHAM BUILT
AN ALTAR THERE AND ARRANGED THE
WOOD ON IT. HE BOUND HIS SON
ISAAC AND LAID HIM ON THE ALTAR,
ON TOP OF THE WOOD. THEN HE
REACHED OUT HIS HAND AND TOOK
THE KNIFE TO SLAY HIS SON."

GENESIS 22:9–10

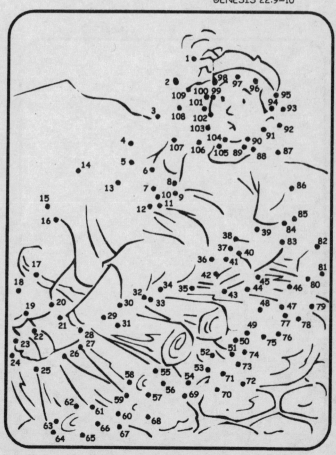

GOD WILL PROVIDE

"BUT THE ANGEL OF THE LORD CALLED OUT TO HIM FROM HEAVEN, 'ABRAHAM! ABRAHAM!'

" 'HERE I AM,' HE REPLIED.

"'DO NOT LAY A HAND ON THE BOY,' HE SAID. 'DO NOT DO ANYTHING TO HIM. NOW I KNOW THAT YOU FEAR GOD, BECAUSE YOU HAVE NOT WITHHELD FROM ME YOUR SON, YOUR ONLY SON.'"

GENESIS 22:11–12

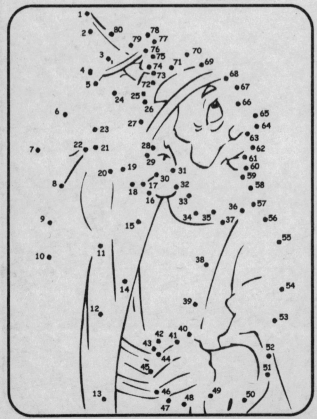

"I WILL PROVIDE"

"ABRAHAM LOOKED UP AND THERE IN A THICKET HE SAW A RAM CAUGHT BY ITS HORNS. HE WENT OVER AND TOOK THE RAM AND SACRIFICED IT AS A BURNT OFFERING INSTEAD OF HIS SON. SO ABRAHAM CALLED THAT PLACE THE LORD WILL PROVIDE. AND TO THIS DAY IT IS SAID, 'ON THE MOUNTAIN OF THE LORD IT WILL BE PROVIDED.'"

GENESIS 22:13–14

ONE AND ONLY SON

"THE ANGEL OF THE LORD CALLED TO ABRAHAM FROM HEAVEN A SECOND TIME AND SAID, 'I SWEAR BY MYSELF, DECLARES THE LORD, THAT BECAUSE YOU HAVE DONE THIS AND HAVE NOT WITHHELD YOUR SON, YOUR ONLY SON, I WILL SURELY BLESS YOU AND MAKE YOUR DESCENDANTS AS NUMEROUS AS THE STARS IN THE SKY AND AS THE SAND ON THE SEASHORE. YOUR DESCENDANTS WILL TAKE POSSESSION OF THE CITIES OF THEIR ENEMIES, AND THROUGH YOUR OFFSPRING ALL NATIONS ON EARTH WILL BE BLESSED, BECAUSE YOU HAVE OBEYED ME.'"

GENESIS 22:15–18

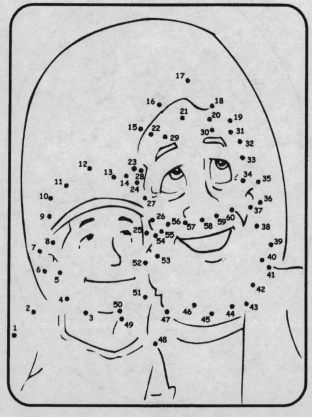

GRAVEYARD

AFTERWARD "ABRAHAM BURIED HIS WIFE SARAH IN THE CAVE IN THE FIELD OF MACHPELAH NEAR MAMRE (WHICH IS AT HEBRON) IN THE LAND OF CANAAN. SO THE FIELD AND THE CAVE IN IT WERE DEEDED TO ABRAHAM BY THE HITTITES AS A BURIAL SITE."

GENESIS 23:19–20

ON MY WAY

"THEN THE SERVANT TOOK TEN OF HIS
MASTER'S CAMELS AND LEFT, TAKING
WITH HIM ALL KINDS OF GOOD THINGS
FROM HIS MASTER. HE SET OUT FOR
ARAM NAHARAIM AND MADE HIS WAY
TO THE TOWN OF NAHOR. HE HAD THE
CAMELS KNEEL DOWN NEAR THE WELL
OUTSIDE THE TOWN; IT WAS TOWARD
EVENING, THE TIME THE WOMEN GO
OUT TO DRAW WATER."

GENESIS 24:10–11

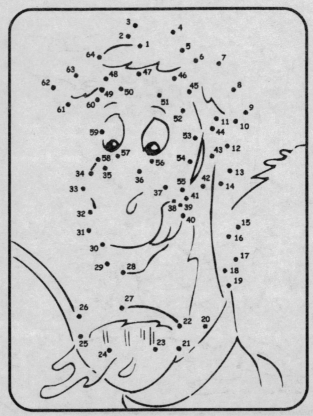

HELP ME, LORD

"THEN HE PRAYED, 'O LORD, GOD OF MY MASTER ABRA-HAM, GIVE ME SUCCESS TODAY, AND SHOW KINDNESS TO MY MASTER ABRAHAM. SEE, I AM STANDING BESIDE THIS SPRING, AND THE DAUGHTERS OF THE TOWNSPEOPLE ARE COMING OUT TO DRAW WATER. MAY IT BE THAT WHEN I SAY TO A GIRL, "PLEASE LET DOWN YOUR JAR THAT I MAY HAVE A DRINK," AND SHE SAYS, "DRINK, AND I'LL WATER YOUR CAMELS TOO"—LET HER BE THE ONE YOU HAVE CHO-SEN FOR YOUR SERVANT ISAAC. BY THIS I WILL KNOW THAT YOU HAVE SHOWN KINDNESS TO MY MASTER."

GENESIS 24:12-14

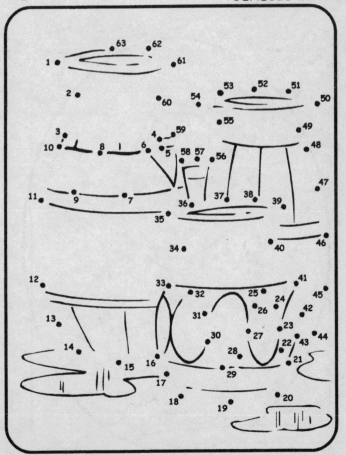

SUCCESS

"AFTER SHE HAD GIVEN HIM A DRINK, SHE SAID, 'I'LL DRAW WATER FOR YOUR CAMELS TOO, UNTIL THEY HAVE FINISHED DRINKING.' SO SHE QUICKLY EMPTIED HER JAR INTO THE TROUGH, RAN BACK TO THE WELL TO DRAW MORE WATER, AND DREW ENOUGH FOR ALL HIS CAMELS. WITHOUT SAYING A WORD, THE MAN WATCHED HER CLOSELY TO LEARN WHETHER OR NOT THE LORD HAD MADE HIS JOURNEY SUCCESSFUL."

GENESIS 24:19-21

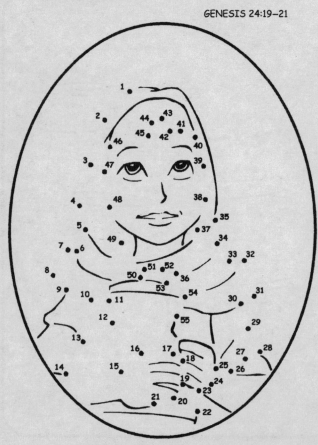

HE LOVED HER

"THEN THE SERVANT TOLD ISAAC ALL HE HAD DONE. ISAAC BROUGHT HER INTO THE TENT OF HIS MOTHER SARAH, AND HE MARRIED REBEKAH. SO SHE BECAME HIS WIFE, AND HE LOVED HER; AND ISAAC WAS COMFORTED AFTER HIS MOTHER'S DEATH."

GENESIS 24:66–67

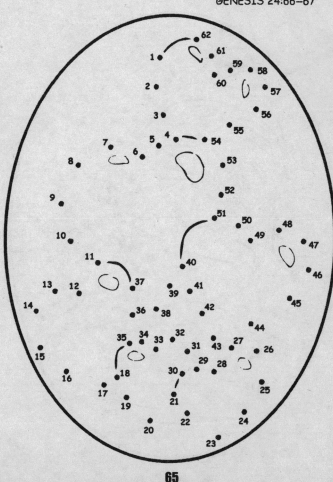

STARTING AGAIN

"ABRAHAM TOOK ANOTHER WIFE, WHOSE NAME WAS KETURAH. SHE BORE HIM ZIMRAN, JOKSHAN, MEDAN, MIDIAN, ISHBAK AND SHUAH."

GENESIS 25:1–2

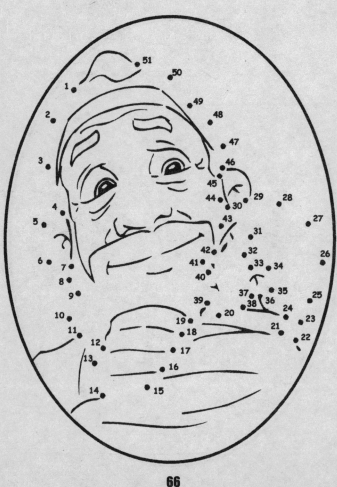

HE GAVE TO ALL

"ABRAHAM LEFT EVERYTHING HE OWNED TO ISAAC. BUT WHILE HE WAS STILL LIVING, HE GAVE GIFTS TO THE SONS OF HIS CONCUBINES AND SENT THEM AWAY FROM HIS SON ISAAC TO THE LAND OF THE EAST."

GENESIS 25:5–6

MY TIME HAS COME

"ALTOGETHER, ABRAHAM LIVED A HUNDRED AND SEVENTY-FIVE YEARS. THEN ABRAHAM BREATHED HIS LAST AND DIED AT A GOOD OLD AGE, AN OLD MAN AND FULL OF YEARS; AND HE WAS GATHERED TO HIS PEOPLE."

GENESIS 25:7–8

BOTH SONS

"HIS SONS ISAAC AND ISHMAEL BURIED HIM IN THE CAVE OF MACHPELAH NEAR MAMRE, IN THE FIELD OF EPHRON SON OF ZOHAR THE HITTITE, THE FIELD ABRAHAM HAD BOUGHT FROM THE HITTITES. THERE ABRAHAM WAS BURIED WITH HIS WIFE SARAH."

GENESIS 25:9–10

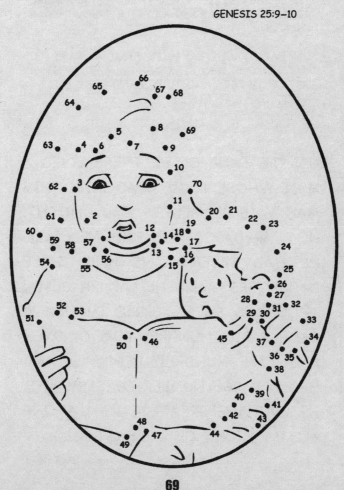

JOB

WELCOME TO THE STORY OF **JOB**: A MAN WHO IS REALLY NOT SO DIFFERENT FROM ANY OF US.

ALTHOUGH WHAT HAPPENED IN JOB'S LIFE TOOK PLACE THOUSANDS OF YEARS AGO, YOU MAY FIND THAT LIFE HAS NOT CHANGED ALL THAT MUCH.

HOPEFULLY, AS YOU READ THE ACCOUNT OF JOB IN YOUR BIBLE, AND AS YOU GO THROUGH THESE ACTIVITIES, YOU WILL LEARN MORE ABOUT GOD AND EVEN A LITTLE ABOUT *YOUR OWN LIFE.*

ON EACH PAGE YOU WILL FIND A MAZE TO PUZZLE YOUR WAY THROUGH—A MAZE WITH A LOT OF TWISTS AND TURNS AND DEAD ENDS— A LOT LIKE LIFE ITSELF.

ENJOY!

"IN THE LAND OF UZ THERE LIVED A MAN WHOSE NAME WAS JOB. THIS MAN WAS BLAMELESS AND UPRIGHT; HE FEARED GOD AND SHUNNED EVIL. HE HAD SEVEN SONS AND THREE DAUGHTERS, AND HE OWNED SEVEN THOUSAND SHEEP, THREE THOUSAND CAMELS, FIVE HUNDRED YOKE OF OXEN AND FIVE HUNDRED DONKEYS, AND HAD A LARGE NUMBER OF SERVANTS. HE WAS THE GREATEST MAN AMONG ALL THE PEOPLE OF THE EAST."

JOB 1:1–3

JOB'S CHILDREN

"HIS SONS USED TO TAKE TURNS HOLDING FEASTS IN THEIR HOMES, AND THEY WOULD INVITE THEIR THREE SISTERS TO EAT AND DRINK WITH THEM. WHEN A PERIOD OF FEASTING HAD RUN ITS COURSE, JOB WOULD SEND AND HAVE THEM PURIFIED. EARLY IN THE MORNING HE WOULD SACRIFICE A BURNT OFFERING FOR EACH OF THEM, THINKING, 'PERHAPS MY CHILDREN HAVE SINNED AND CURSED GOD IN THEIR HEARTS.' THIS WAS JOB'S REGULAR CUSTOM."

JOB 1:4–5

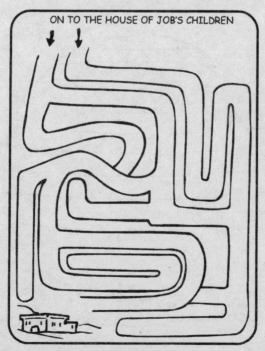

ON TO THE HOUSE OF JOB'S CHILDREN

ANGELS AND SATAN

"ONE DAY THE ANGELS CAME TO PRESENT THEMSELVES BEFORE THE LORD, AND SATAN ALSO CAME WITH THEM. THE LORD SAID TO SATAN, 'WHERE HAVE YOU COME FROM?' SATAN ANSWERED THE LORD, 'FROM ROAMING THROUGH THE EARTH AND GOING BACK AND FORTH IN IT.'"

JOB 1:6–7

As you go through the maze, collect the letters and unscramble them.

— — — — — —

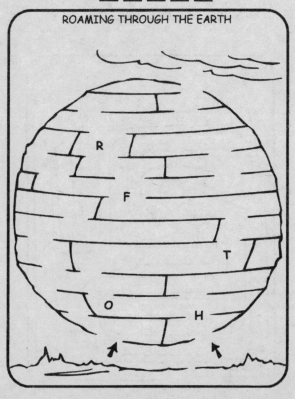

ROAMING THROUGH THE EARTH

BLAMELESS AND UPRIGHT

"THEN THE LORD SAID TO SATAN, 'HAVE YOU CONSIDERED MY SERVANT JOB? THERE IS NO ONE ON EARTH LIKE HIM; HE IS BLAMELESS AND UPRIGHT, A MAN WHO FEARS GOD AND SHUNS EVIL.'"

JOB 1:8

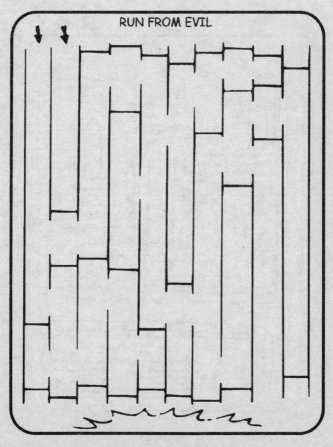

RUN FROM EVIL

REMOVE YOUR HEDGE

"'DOES JOB FEAR GOD FOR NOTHING?' SATAN REPLIED. 'HAVE YOU NOT PUT A HEDGE AROUND HIM AND HIS HOUSEHOLD AND EVERYTHING HE HAS? YOU HAVE BLESSED THE WORK OF HIS HANDS, SO THAT HIS FLOCKS AND HERDS ARE SPREAD THROUGHOUT THE LAND. BUT STRETCH OUT YOUR HAND AND STRIKE EVERYTHING HE HAS, AND HE WILL SURELY CURSE YOU TO YOUR FACE.'"

JOB 1:9–11

THROUGH THE HEDGE

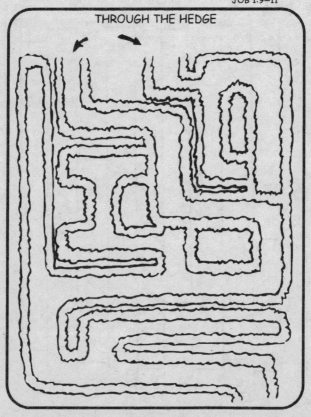

DON'T LAY A FINGER

"THE LORD SAID TO SATAN, 'VERY WELL, THEN, EVERYTHING HE HAS IS IN YOUR HANDS, BUT ON THE MAN HIMSELF DO NOT LAY A FINGER.' THEN SATAN WENT OUT FROM THE PRESENCE OF THE LORD."

JOB 1:12

OUT FROM GOD'S PRESENCE

THE TESTING BEGINS

"ONE DAY WHEN JOB'S SONS AND DAUGHTERS WERE FEASTING AND DRINKING WINE AT THE OLDEST BROTHER'S HOUSE, A MESSENGER CAME TO JOB AND SAID, 'THE OXEN WERE PLOWING AND THE DONKEYS WERE GRAZING NEARBY, AND THE SABEANS ATTACKED AND CARRIED THEM OFF. THEY PUT THE SERVANTS TO THE SWORD, AND I AM THE ONLY ONE WHO HAS ESCAPED TO TELL YOU!'"

JOB 1:13–15

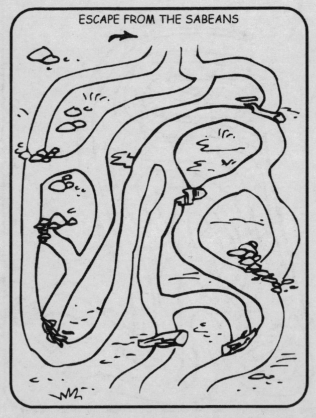

ESCAPE FROM THE SABEANS

ANOTHER MESSENGER

"WHILE HE WAS STILL SPEAKING, ANOTHER MESSENGER CAME AND SAID, 'THE FIRE OF GOD FELL FROM THE SKY AND BURNED UP THE SHEEP AND THE SERVANTS, AND I AM THE ONLY ONE WHO HAS ESCAPED TO TELL YOU!'"

JOB 1:16

As you go through the maze, collect the letters and unscramble them.

_ _ _ _ _ _ _

FIRE FROM THE SKY

RAIDING PARTIES

"WHILE HE WAS STILL SPEAKING, ANOTHER MESSENGER CAME AND SAID, 'THE CHALDEANS FORMED THREE RAIDING PARTIES AND SWEPT DOWN ON YOUR CAMELS AND CARRIED THEM OFF. THEY PUT THE SERVANTS TO THE SWORD, AND I AM THE ONLY ONE WHO HAS ESCAPED TO TELL YOU!'"

JOB 1:17

ESCAPE THE RAIDERS!

MY CHILDREN

"WHILE HE WAS STILL SPEAKING, YET ANOTHER MESSENGER CAME AND SAID, 'YOUR SONS AND DAUGHTERS WERE FEASTING AND DRINKING WINE AT THE OLDEST BROTHER'S HOUSE, WHEN SUDDENLY A MIGHTY WIND SWEPT IN FROM THE DESERT AND STRUCK THE FOUR CORNERS OF THE HOUSE. IT COLLAPSED ON THEM AND THEY ARE DEAD, AND I AM THE ONLY ONE WHO HAS ESCAPED TO TELL YOU!'"

JOB 1:18–19

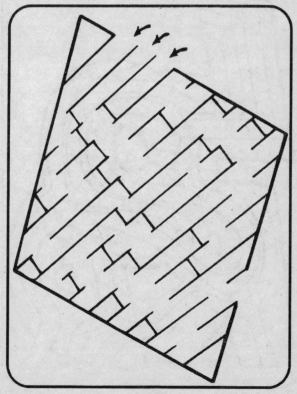

I WILL PRAISE HIM

"AT THIS, JOB GOT UP AND TORE HIS ROBE AND SHAVED HIS HEAD. THEN HE FELL TO THE GROUND IN WORSHIP AND SAID: 'NAKED I CAME FROM MY MOTHER'S WOMB, AND NAKED I WILL DEPART. THE LORD GAVE AND THE LORD HAS TAKEN AWAY; MAY THE NAME OF THE LORD BE PRAISED.'"

JOB 1:20–21

As you go through the maze, collect the letters and unscramble them. — — — — — —

PRAISE THE LORD

JOB PASSES

"IN ALL THIS, JOB DID NOT SIN BY CHARGING GOD WITH WRONGDOING."

JOB 1:22

As you go through the maze, collect the letters and unscramble them.

_ _ _ _

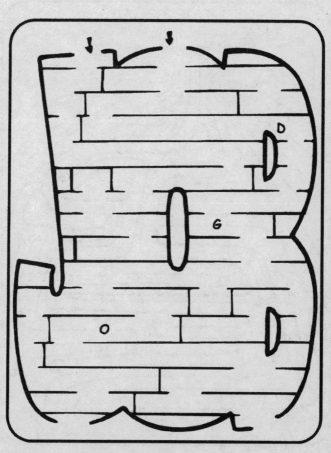

BEFORE GOD

"ON ANOTHER DAY THE ANGELS CAME
TO PRESENT THEMSELVES BEFORE THE
LORD, AND SATAN ALSO CAME WITH
THEM TO PRESENT HIMSELF BEFORE
HIM."

JOB 2:1

BEFORE THE LORD

INTEGRITY

"THEN THE LORD SAID TO SATAN, 'HAVE YOU CONSIDERED MY SERVANT JOB? THERE IS NO ONE ON EARTH LIKE HIM; HE IS BLAMELESS AND UPRIGHT, A MAN WHO FEARS GOD AND SHUNS EVIL. AND HE STILL MAINTAINS HIS INTEGRITY, THOUGH YOU INCITED ME AGAINST HIM TO RUIN HIM WITHOUT ANY REASON.'"

JOB 2:3

As you go through the maze, collect the letters and unscramble them. _ _ _ _ _

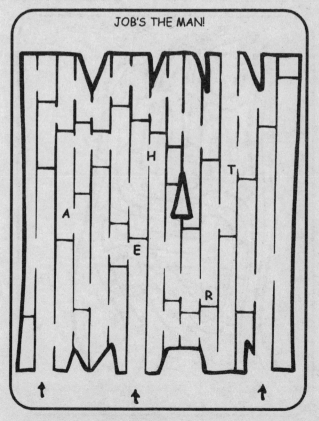

JOB'S THE MAN!

SKIN FOR SKIN

"'SKIN FOR SKIN!' SATAN REPLIED. 'A MAN WILL GIVE ALL HE HAS FOR HIS OWN LIFE. BUT STRETCH OUT YOUR HAND AND STRIKE HIS FLESH AND BONES, AND HE WILL SURELY CURSE YOU TO YOUR FACE.'"THE LORD SAID TO SATAN, 'VERY WELL, THEN, HE IS IN YOUR HANDS; BUT YOU MUST SPARE HIS LIFE.'"

JOB 2:4–6

As you go through the maze, collect the letters and unscramble them. ___ ___ ___ ___ ___ ___ ___

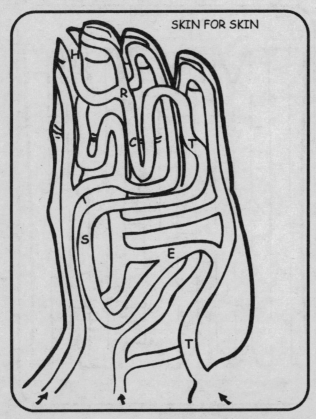

SKIN FOR SKIN

SECOND TEST

"SO SATAN WENT OUT FROM THE PRESENCE OF THE LORD AND AFFLICTED JOB WITH PAINFUL SORES FROM THE SOLES OF HIS FEET TO THE TOP OF HIS HEAD. THEN JOB TOOK A PIECE OF BROKEN POTTERY AND SCRAPED HIMSELF WITH IT AS HE SAT AMONG THE ASHES. HIS WIFE SAID TO HIM, 'ARE YOU STILL HOLDING ON TO YOUR INTEGRITY? CURSE GOD AND DIE!'"

JOB 2:7–9

OFF TO THE ASH HEAP

TALKING FOOLISHLY

"HE REPLIED, 'YOU ARE TALKING LIKE A
FOOLISH WOMAN. SHALL WE ACCEPT
GOOD FROM GOD, AND NOT TROUBLE?'
IN ALL THIS, JOB DID NOT SIN IN
WHAT HE SAID."

JOB 2:10

As you go through the maze, collect
the letters and unscramble them.   _ _ _ _ _ _ _ _

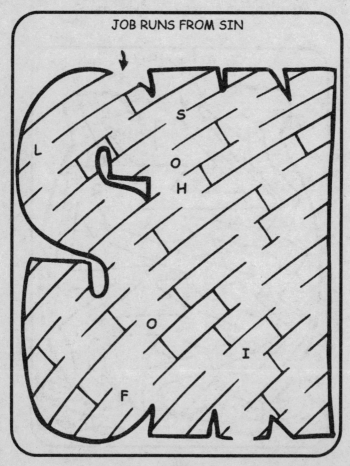

JOB RUNS FROM SIN

FRIENDS

"WHEN JOB'S THREE FRIENDS, ELIPHAZ THE TEMANITE, BILDAD THE SHUHITE AND ZOPHAR THE NAAMATHITE, HEARD ABOUT ALL THE TROUBLES THAT HAD COME UPON HIM, THEY SET OUT FROM THEIR HOMES AND MET TOGETHER BY AGREEMENT TO GO AND SYMPATHIZE WITH HIM AND COMFORT HIM."

JOB 2:11

As you go through the maze, collect the letters and unscramble them.

___ ___ ___ ___ ___

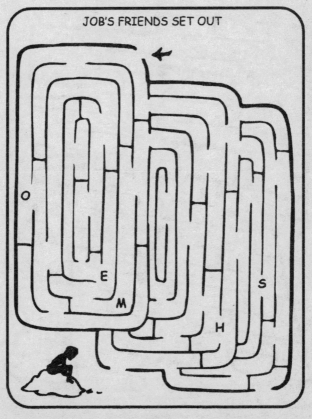

JOB'S FRIENDS SET OUT

FEAR AND DREAD

"'WHAT I FEARED HAS COME UPON ME;
WHAT I DREADED HAS HAPPENED TO
ME. I HAVE NO PEACE, NO QUIETNESS;
I HAVE NO REST, BUT ONLY TURMOIL.'"

JOB 3:25–26

As you go through the maze, collect
the letters and unscramble them. — — — — —

GOING THROUGH FEAR

ELIPHAZ

"THEN ELIPHAZ THE TEMANITE REPLIED: 'IF SOMEONE VENTURES A WORD WITH YOU, WILL YOU BE IMPATIENT? BUT WHO CAN KEEP FROM SPEAKING? THINK HOW YOU HAVE INSTRUCTED MANY, HOW YOU HAVE STRENGTHENED FEEBLE HANDS.'"

JOB 4:1–3

FEEBLE HANDS

MORTAL MAN AND GOD

"'"CAN A MORTAL BE MORE RIGHTEOUS THAN GOD? CAN A MAN BE MORE PURE THAN HIS MAKER?"'"

"'BUT IF IT WERE I, I WOULD APPEAL TO GOD; I WOULD LAY MY CAUSE BEFORE HIM. HE PERFORMS WONDERS THAT CANNOT BE FATHOMED, MIRACLES THAT CANNOT BE COUNTED.'"

JOB 4:17; 5:8-9

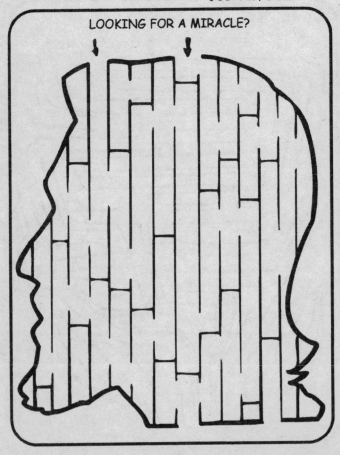

LOOKING FOR A MIRACLE?

JOB ANSWERS ELIPHAZ

"THEN JOB REPLIED: 'IF ONLY MY ANGUISH COULD BE WEIGHED AND ALL MY MISERY BE PLACED ON THE SCALES!'"

JOB 6:1–2

As you go through the maze, collect the letters and unscramble them.

— — — — — — — —

GRANT MY REQUEST

"'OH, THAT I MIGHT HAVE MY REQUEST,
THAT GOD WOULD GRANT WHAT I HOPE
FOR, THAT GOD WOULD BE WILLING
TO CRUSH ME, TO LET LOOSE HIS HAND
AND CUT ME OFF!'"

JOB 6:8–9

WHAT HOPE ?

"'WHAT STRENGTH DO I HAVE, THAT I SHOULD STILL HOPE? WHAT PROSPECTS, THAT I SHOULD BE PATIENT?'"

JOB 6:11

As you go through the maze, collect the letters and unscramble them.

_ _ _ _ _ _ _ _ _

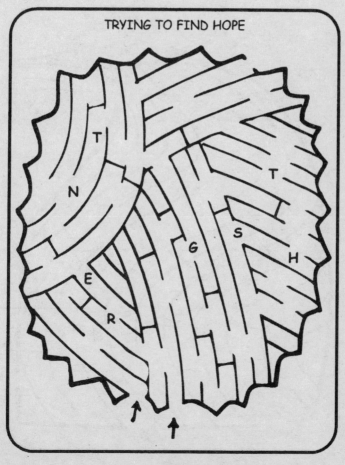

TRYING TO FIND HOPE

NO POWER IN ME

"'DO I HAVE ANY POWER TO HELP MYSELF, NOW THAT SUCCESS HAS BEEN DRIVEN FROM ME? A DESPAIRING MAN SHOULD HAVE THE DEVOTION OF HIS FRIENDS, EVEN THOUGH HE FORSAKES THE FEAR OF THE ALMIGHTY.'"

JOB 6:13-14

DRIVEN FROM SUCCESS

TEACH ME

"'TEACH ME, AND I WILL BE QUIET; SHOW ME WHERE I HAVE BEEN WRONG. HOW PAINFUL ARE HONEST WORDS! BUT WHAT DO YOUR ARGUMENTS PROVE?'"

JOB 6:24–25

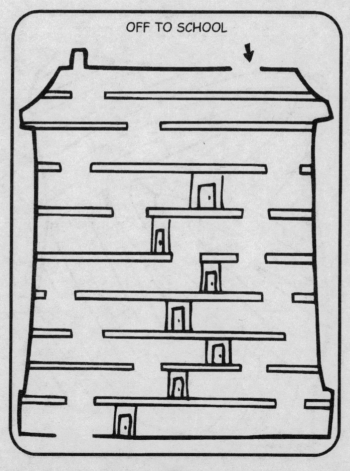

OFF TO SCHOOL

WHAT IS MAN?

"'WHAT IS MAN THAT YOU MAKE SO MUCH OF HIM, THAT YOU GIVE HIM SO MUCH ATTENTION, THAT YOU EXAMINE HIM EVERY MORNING AND TEST HIM EVERY MOMENT?'"

JOB 7:17–18

As you go through the maze, collect the letters and unscramble them.

— — — —

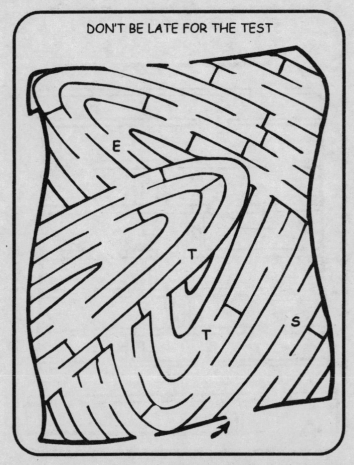

DON'T BE LATE FOR THE TEST

AM I A BURDEN?

"'IF I HAVE SINNED, WHAT HAVE I DONE TO YOU, O WATCHER OF MEN? WHY HAVE YOU MADE ME YOUR TARGET? HAVE I BECOME A BURDEN TO YOU?'"

JOB 7:20

As you go through the maze, collect the letters and unscramble them. _ _ _ _ _ _

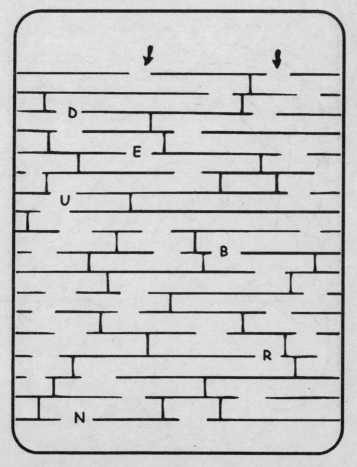

PARDON ME

"'WHY DO YOU NOT PARDON MY OFFENSES AND FORGIVE MY SINS? FOR I WILL SOON LIE DOWN IN THE DUST; YOU WILL SEARCH FOR ME, BUT I WILL BE NO MORE.'"

JOB 7:21

As you go through the maze, collect the letters and unscramble them. _ _ _ _ _ _ _

LOOKING FOR A PLACE TO LIE DOWN

BILDAD

"THEN BILDAD THE SHUHITE REPLIED: 'HOW LONG WILL YOU SAY SUCH THINGS? YOUR WORDS ARE A BLUSTERING WIND. DOES GOD PERVERT JUSTICE? DOES THE ALMIGHTY PERVERT WHAT IS RIGHT?'"

JOB 8:1–3

A BLUSTERING WIND

LOOK TO GOD

"'BUT IF YOU WILL LOOK TO GOD AND
PLEAD WITH THE ALMIGHTY, IF YOU
ARE PURE AND UPRIGHT, EVEN NOW
HE WILL ROUSE HIMSELF ON YOUR
BEHALF AND RESTORE YOU TO YOUR
RIGHTFUL PLACE.'"

JOB 8:5–6

As you go through the maze, collect
the letters and unscramble them. —— —— —— —— —— —— ——

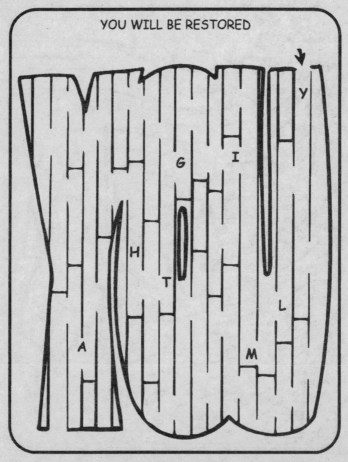

YOU WILL BE RESTORED

SHOUTS OF JOY

"'SURELY GOD DOES NOT REJECT A BLAMELESS MAN OR STRENGTHEN THE HANDS OF EVILDOERS. HE WILL YET FILL YOUR MOUTH WITH LAUGHTER AND YOUR LIPS WITH SHOUTS OF JOY.'"

JOB 8:20–21

As you go through the maze, collect the letters and unscramble them.

___ ___ ___ ___ ___

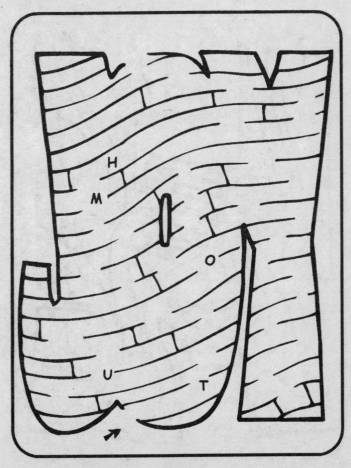

YOU GAVE ME LIFE

"'YOU GAVE ME LIFE AND SHOWED ME KINDNESS, AND IN YOUR PROVIDENCE WATCHED OVER MY SPIRIT. BUT THIS IS WHAT YOU CONCEALED IN YOUR HEART, AND I KNOW THAT THIS WAS IN YOUR MIND.'"

JOB 10:12–13

ZOPHAR

"THEN ZOPHAR THE NAAMATHITE REPLIED: 'ARE ALL THESE WORDS TO GO UNANSWERED? IS THIS TALKER TO BE VINDICATED? WILL YOUR IDLE TALK REDUCE MEN TO SILENCE? WILL NO ONE REBUKE YOU WHEN YOU MOCK?'"

JOB 11:1–3

As you go through the maze, collect the letters and unscramble them. _ _ _ _ _ _

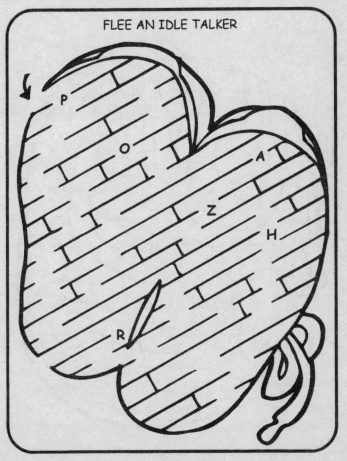

FLEE AN IDLE TALKER

MY BELIEFS

"'YOU SAY TO GOD, "MY BELIEFS ARE FLAWLESS AND I AM PURE IN YOUR SIGHT." OH, HOW I WISH THAT GOD WOULD SPEAK, THAT HE WOULD OPEN HIS LIPS AGAINST YOU.'"

JOB 11:4–5

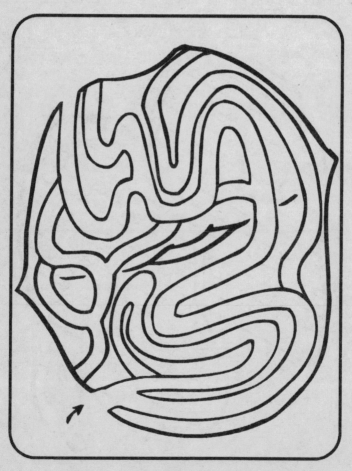

CONFESS

"'YET IF YOU DEVOTE YOUR HEART TO HIM AND STRETCH OUT YOUR HANDS TO HIM, IF YOU PUT AWAY THE SIN THAT IS IN YOUR HAND AND ALLOW NO EVIL TO DWELL IN YOUR TENT, THEN YOU WILL LIFT UP YOUR FACE WITHOUT SHAME; YOU WILL STAND FIRM AND WITHOUT FEAR.'"

JOB 11:13–15

THE ALMIGHTY

"'WHAT YOU KNOW, I ALSO KNOW;
I AM NOT INFERIOR TO YOU.
BUT I DESIRE TO SPEAK TO THE
ALMIGHTY AND TO ARGUE MY CASE
WITH GOD.'"

JOB 13:2-3

As you go through the maze, collect
the letters and unscramble them. _ _ _ _ _

GO MAKE YOUR ARGUMENT

BE SILENT

"'YOU, HOWEVER, SMEAR ME WITH LIES; YOU ARE WORTHLESS PHYSICIANS, ALL OF YOU! IF ONLY YOU WOULD BE ALTOGETHER SILENT! FOR YOU, THAT WOULD BE WISDOM.'"

JOB 13:4–5

As you go through the maze, collect the letters and unscramble them. _ _ _ _ _ _

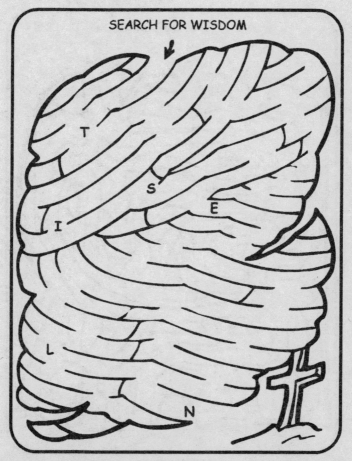

SEARCH FOR WISDOM

INNOCENT

"'KEEP SILENT AND LET ME SPEAK; THEN LET COME TO ME WHAT MAY.'"

"'LISTEN CAREFULLY TO MY WORDS; LET YOUR EARS TAKE IN WHAT I SAY. NOW THAT I HAVE PREPARED MY CASE, I KNOW I WILL BE VINDICATED.'"

JOB 13:13, 17–18

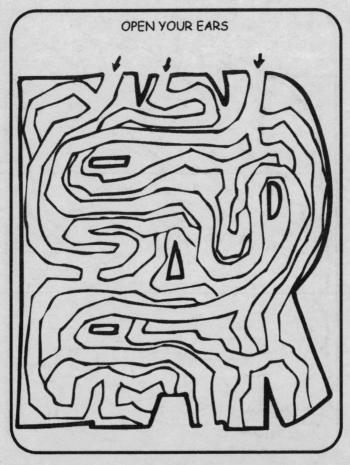

OPEN YOUR EARS

LONG-WINDED

"'I HAVE HEARD MANY THINGS LIKE THESE; MISERABLE COMFORTERS ARE YOU ALL! WILL YOUR LONG-WINDED SPEECHES NEVER END? WHAT AILS YOU THAT YOU KEEP ON ARGUING?'"

JOB 16:2–3

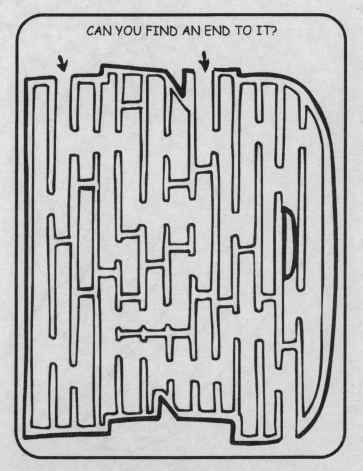

CAN YOU FIND AN END TO IT?

FINE SPEECHES

"'I ALSO COULD SPEAK LIKE YOU, IF YOU WERE IN MY PLACE; I COULD MAKE FINE SPEECHES AGAINST YOU AND SHAKE MY HEAD AT YOU.'"

JOB 16:4

As you go through the maze, collect the letters and unscramble them. _ _ _ _ _

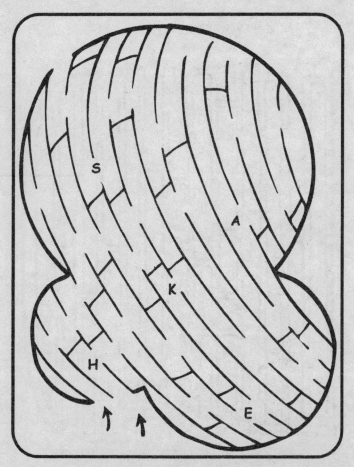

REDEEMER

"'I KNOW THAT MY REDEEMER LIVES, AND THAT IN THE END HE WILL STAND UPON THE EARTH. AND AFTER MY SKIN HAS BEEN DESTROYED, YET IN MY FLESH I WILL SEE GOD.'"

JOB 19:25–26

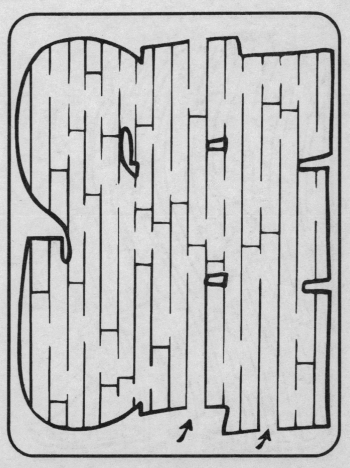

ELIPHAZ

"THEN ELIPHAZ THE TEMANITE REPLIED: 'CAN A MAN BE OF BENEFIT TO GOD? CAN EVEN A WISE MAN BENEFIT HIM?'"

JOB 22:1–2

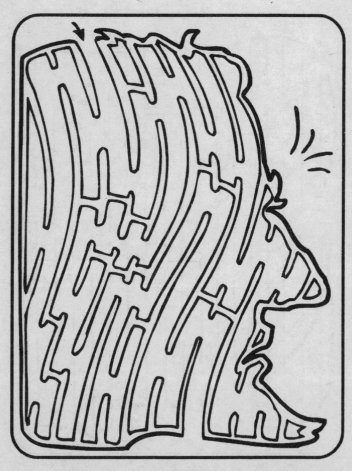

STILL NOT LISTENING

"'YOU DEMANDED SECURITY FROM YOUR BROTHERS FOR NO REASON; YOU STRIPPED MEN OF THEIR CLOTHING, LEAVING THEM NAKED.'"

"'SUBMIT TO GOD AND BE AT PEACE WITH HIM; IN THIS WAY PROSPERITY WILL COME TO YOU.'"

JOB 22:6, 21

WAITING FOR PROSPERITY

HE KNOWS ME

"'BUT HE KNOWS THE WAY THAT I TAKE; WHEN HE HAS TESTED ME, I WILL COME FORTH AS GOLD.'"

"'AS LONG AS I HAVE LIFE WITHIN ME, THE BREATH OF GOD IN MY NOSTRILS, MY LIPS WILL NOT SPEAK WICKEDNESS, AND MY TONGUE WILL UTTER NO DECEIT.'"

JOB 23:10; 27:3-4

TRYING TO FIND GOLD?

INTEGRITY

"'I WILL NEVER ADMIT YOU ARE IN THE RIGHT; TILL I DIE, I WILL NOT DENY MY INTEGRITY. I WILL MAINTAIN MY RIGHTEOUSNESS AND NEVER LET GO OF IT; MY CONSCIENCE WILL NOT REPROACH ME AS LONG AS I LIVE.'"

JOB 27:5–6

As you go through the maze, collect the letters and unscramble them.   __ __ __ __ __

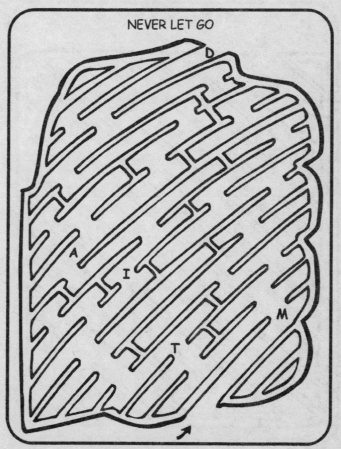

NEVER LET GO

FEAR THE LORD

"'AND HE SAID TO MAN, THE FEAR OF THE LORD—THAT IS WISDOM, AND TO SHUN EVIL IS UNDERSTANDING.'"

JOB 28:28

As you go through the maze, collect the letters and unscramble them.

_ _ _ _ _ _

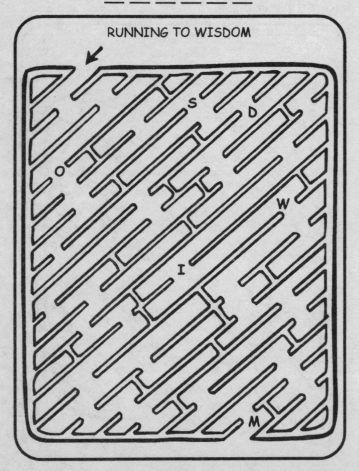

RUNNING TO WISDOM

BLAMELESS

"'IF I HAVE WALKED IN FALSEHOOD OR MY FOOT HAS HURRIED AFTER DECEIT—LET GOD WEIGH ME IN HONEST SCALES AND HE WILL KNOW THAT I AM BLAMELESS—IF MY STEPS HAVE TURNED FROM THE PATH, IF MY HEART HAS BEEN LED BY MY EYES, OR IF MY HANDS HAVE BEEN DEFILED, THEN MAY OTHERS EAT WHAT I HAVE SOWN, AND MAY MY CROPS BE UPROOTED.'"

JOB 31:5–8

ON THE PATH TO TRUTH

ANGRY WITH JOB

"SO THESE THREE MEN STOPPED ANSWERING JOB, BECAUSE HE WAS RIGHTEOUS IN HIS OWN EYES. BUT ELIHU SON OF BARAKEL THE BUZITE, OF THE FAMILY OF RAM, BECAME VERY ANGRY WITH JOB FOR JUSTIFYING HIMSELF RATHER THAN GOD."

JOB 32:1-2

As you go through the maze, collect the letters and unscramble them. _ _ _ _ _ _

LOOKING FOR ANSWERS

NOTHING MORE TO SAY

"HE WAS ALSO ANGRY WITH THE THREE FRIENDS, BECAUSE THEY HAD FOUND NO WAY TO REFUTE JOB, AND YET HAD CONDEMNED HIM. NOW ELIHU HAD WAITED BEFORE SPEAKING TO JOB BECAUSE THEY WERE OLDER THAN HE. BUT WHEN HE SAW THAT THE THREE MEN HAD NOTHING MORE TO SAY, HIS ANGER WAS AROUSED."

JOB 32:3–5

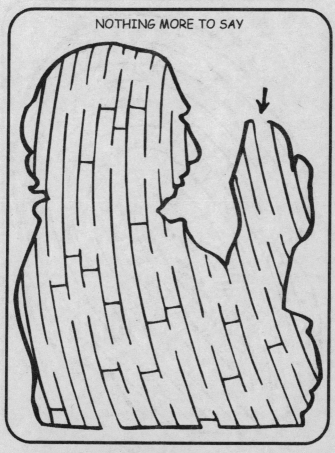

NOTHING MORE TO SAY

JOB SPEAKS OUT

"JOB SAYS, 'I AM INNOCENT, BUT GOD DENIES ME JUSTICE. ALTHOUGH I AM RIGHT, I AM CONSIDERED A LIAR; ALTHOUGH I AM GUILTLESS, HIS ARROW INFLICTS AN INCURABLE WOUND.'"

JOB 34:5–6

ELIHU ANSWERS JOB

"'HOW MUCH LESS, THEN, WILL HE LISTEN WHEN YOU SAY THAT YOU DO NOT SEE HIM, THAT YOUR CASE IS BEFORE HIM AND YOU MUST WAIT FOR HIM, AND FURTHER, THAT HIS ANGER NEVER PUNISHES AND HE DOES NOT TAKE THE LEAST NOTICE OF WICKEDNESS.'"

JOB 35:14–15

As you go through the maze, collect the letters and unscramble them. _ _ _ _ _

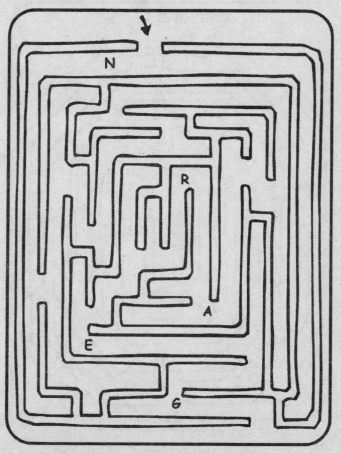

REFUSING TO REPENT

"'SHOULD GOD THEN REWARD YOU ON YOUR TERMS, WHEN YOU REFUSE TO REPENT? YOU MUST DECIDE, NOT I; SO TELL ME WHAT YOU KNOW.'"

JOB 34:33

SEARCHING FOR REWARD

EMPTY TALK

"'SO JOB OPENS HIS MOUTH WITH EMPTY TALK; WITHOUT KNOWLEDGE HE MULTIPLIES WORDS. BEAR WITH ME A LITTLE LONGER AND I WILL SHOW YOU THAT THERE IS MORE TO BE SAID IN GOD'S BEHALF.'"

JOB 35:16–36:2

EMPTY TALK

THE LORD ANSWERS

"THEN THE LORD ANSWERED JOB OUT OF THE STORM. HE SAID: 'WHO IS THIS THAT DARKENS MY COUNSEL WITH WORDS WITHOUT KNOWLEDGE?'"

JOB 38:1–2

As you go through the maze, collect the letters and unscramble them.

_ _ _ _ _ _ _ _

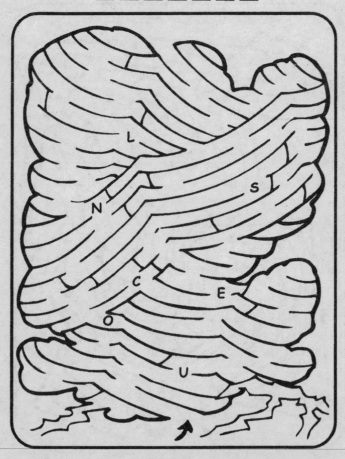

YOU WILL ANSWER ME

"'BRACE YOURSELF LIKE A MAN; I WILL QUESTION YOU, AND YOU SHALL ANSWER ME. WHERE WERE YOU WHEN I LAID THE EARTH'S FOUNDATION? TELL ME, IF YOU UNDERSTAND.'"

JOB 38:3–4

WHERE IS THE EARTH'S FOUNDATION?

ANSWER GOD

"THE LORD SAID TO JOB: 'WILL THE ONE WHO CONTENDS WITH THE ALMIGHTY CORRECT HIM? LET HIM WHO ACCUSES GOD ANSWER HIM!'"

JOB 40:1–2

As you go through the maze, collect the letters and unscramble them.

_ _ _ _ _ _ _ _

WOULD YOU CORRECT HIM?

JOB ANSWERS GOD

"THEN JOB ANSWERED THE LORD: 'I AM UNWORTHY—HOW CAN I REPLY TO YOU? I PUT MY HAND OVER MY MOUTH. I SPOKE ONCE, BUT I HAVE NO ANSWER—TWICE, BUT I WILL SAY NO MORE.'"

JOB 40:3–5

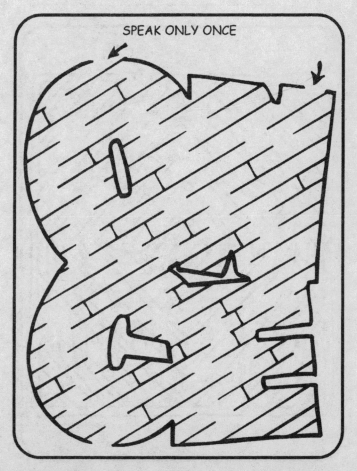

SPEAK ONLY ONCE

ANYTHING IS POSSIBLE

"THEN JOB REPLIED TO THE LORD: 'I KNOW THAT YOU CAN DO ALL THINGS; NO PLAN OF YOURS CAN BE THWARTED.'"

JOB 42:1-2

As you go through the maze, collect the letters and unscramble them.

_ _ _ _ _ _ _ _ _ _

COLOR THE PICTURE

JUST FOR FUN, LET'S HAVE A LOOK AT THE *CREATURES OF THE BIBLE.* FROM ANIMALS TO INSECTS, TO CREATURES THAT SWIM IN THE SEA OR SLITHER ON THE GROUND, THE WORD OF GOD JUST ABOUT COVERS THEM ALL.

WE WILL SEE THAT ANIMALS WERE AN IMPORTANT PART OF PEOPLES' LIVES BACK IN THE TIME THAT THE BOOKS OF THE BIBLE WERE WRITTEN.

MANY TIMES, WE WILL FIND THAT THE BIBLE EVEN COMPARES *US* TO ANIMALS AS IT TRIES TO HELP US DISCOVER TRUTHS ABOUT OURSELVES.

FiNiSH THE PiCTURE

COMPLETE THE PICTURE BY DUPLICATING THE
FINISHED HALF ONTO THE UNFINISHED AREA.

"THE LORD HARDENED THE HEART
OF PHARAOH KING OF EGYPT, SO THAT
HE PURSUED THE ISRAELITES, WHO
WERE MARCHING OUT BOLDLY. THE
EGYPTIANS—ALL PHARAOH'S *HORSES*
AND CHARIOTS, HORSEMEN AND
TROOPS—PURSUED THE ISRAELITES
AND OVERTOOK THEM AS THEY CAMPED
BY THE SEA NEAR PI HAHIROTH,
OPPOSITE BAAL ZEPHON."

EXODUS 14:8–9

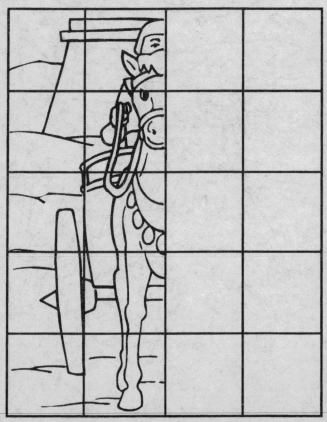

COPY THE PICTURE

USING THE GRID, DRAW THE PICTURE BELOW.

PiCTURE PiECES

PUT THE PICTURE PIECES IN THE RIGHT ORDER. DRAW WHAT IS IN EACH NUMBERED BOX BELOW INTO EACH BOX OF THE SAME NUMBER.

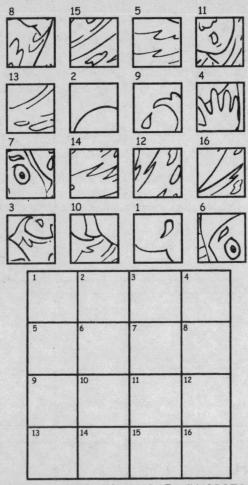

"WHEN PHARAOH'S *HORSES*, CHARIOTS AND HORSEMEN WENT INTO THE SEA, THE LORD BROUGHT THE WATERS OF THE SEA BACK OVER THEM, BUT THE ISRAELITES WALKED THROUGH THE SEA ON DRY GROUND."

EXODUS 15:19

MISSING PIECES

Does the picture look a little unfinished to you? A lot of things are left out, but you can finish it by filling in as many missing pieces as you can find. Look carefully!

"THEY CAME OUT WITH ALL THEIR TROOPS AND A LARGE NUMBER OF *HORSES* AND CHARIOTS—A HUGE ARMY, AS NUMEROUS AS THE SAND ON THE SEASHORE. ALL THESE KINGS JOINED FORCES AND MADE CAMP TOGETHER AT THE WATERS OF MEROM, TO FIGHT AGAINST ISRAEL."

JOSHUA 11:4–5

WHAT'S DIFFERENT?

Look carefully at the pictures below. They look the same at first glance, but. . .are they? Circle any differences you find.

"IN THE COURSE OF TIME, ABSALOM PROVIDED HIMSELF WITH A CHARIOT AND *HORSES* AND WITH FIFTY MEN TO RUN AHEAD OF HIM."

2 SAMUEL 15:1

HIDDEN LETTERS

Look carefully at the picture below. Then color in the areas that contain a square to reveal the hidden letters. Then use the letters to complete the verse below.

"AS THEY WERE WALKING ALONG AND TALKING TOGETHER, SUDDENLY A CHARIOT OF FIRE AND _ _ _ _ _ _ OF FIRE APPEARED AND SEPARATED THE TWO OF THEM, AND ELIJAH WENT UP TO HEAVEN IN A WHIRLWIND."

2 KINGS 2:11

_ _ _ _ _ _

COPY THE PICTURE

USING THE GRID, DRAW THE PICTURE BELOW.

FLEECE AS WHITE AS SNOW

COLOR THE PICTURE

"THERE HE SAW A WELL IN THE FIELD, WITH THREE FLOCKS OF *SHEEP* LYING NEAR IT BECAUSE THE FLOCKS WERE WATERED FROM THAT WELL. THE STONE OVER THE MOUTH OF THE WELL WAS LARGE."

GENESIS 29:2

PiCTURE PiECES

PUT THE PICTURE PIECES IN THE RIGHT ORDER. DRAW WHAT IS IN EACH NUMBERED BOX BELOW INTO EACH BOX OF THE SAME NUMBER.

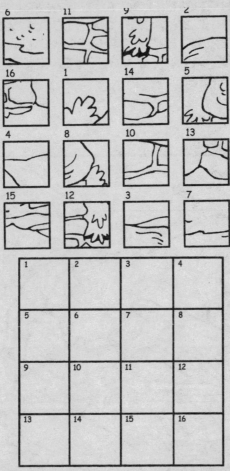

"WHEN ALL THE FLOCKS WERE GATHERED THERE, THE SHEPHERDS WOULD ROLL THE STONE AWAY FROM THE WELL'S MOUTH AND WATER THE *SHEEP*. THEN THEY WOULD RETURN THE STONE TO ITS PLACE OVER THE MOUTH OF THE WELL."

GENESIS 29:3

WHAT'S DIFFERENT?

Look carefully at the pictures below. They look the same at first glance, but. . .are they? Circle any differences you find.

"WHILE HE WAS STILL TALKING WITH THEM, RACHEL CAME WITH HER FATHER'S *SHEEP*, FOR SHE WAS A SHEPHERDESS."

GENESIS 29:9

FiNiSH THE PiCTURE

Complete the picture by duplicating the finished half onto the unfinished area.

"'LET ME GO THROUGH ALL YOUR FLOCKS TODAY AND REMOVE FROM THEM EVERY SPECKLED OR SPOTTED *SHEEP*, EVERY DARK-COLORED LAMB AND EVERY SPOTTED OR SPECKLED GOAT. THEY WILL BE MY WAGES.'"

GENESIS 30:32

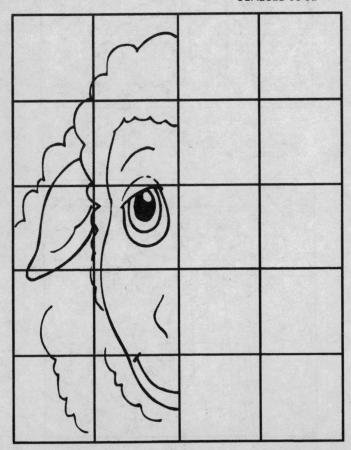

MISSING PIECES

Does the picture look a little unfinished to you? A lot of things are left out, but you can finish it by filling in as many missing pieces as you can find. Look carefully!

"DAVID SAID TO GOD, 'WAS IT NOT I WHO ORDERED THE FIGHTING MEN TO BE COUNTED? I AM THE ONE WHO HAS SINNED AND DONE WRONG. THESE ARE BUT *SHEEP*. WHAT HAVE THEY DONE? O LORD MY GOD, LET YOUR HAND FALL UPON ME AND MY FAMILY, BUT DO NOT LET THIS PLAGUE REMAIN ON YOUR PEOPLE.'"

1 CHRONICLES 21:17

HIDDEN LETTERS

Color in the areas that contain a square to reveal the hidden letters. Then use the letters to complete the verse below.

"BUT HE BROUGHT HIS PEOPLE OUT
    LIKE A FLOCK;
    HE LED THEM LIKE __ __ __ __ __
    THROUGH THE DESERT.
HE GUIDED THEM SAFELY, SO THEY
    WERE UNAFRAID;
    BUT THE SEA ENGULFED THEIR
    ENEMIES."

PSALM 78:52–53

____ ____ ____ ____ ____

COPY THE PICTURE

USING THE GRID, DRAW THE PICTURE BELOW.

BILLY IS HIS NAME

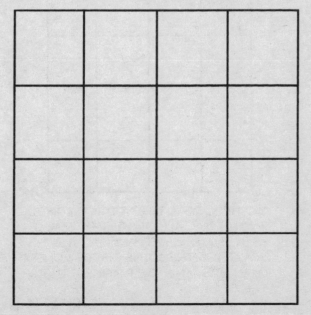

PICTURE PIECES

PUT THE PICTURE PIECES IN THE RIGHT ORDER.
DRAW WHAT IS IN EACH NUMBERED BOX
BELOW INTO EACH BOX OF THE SAME NUMBER.

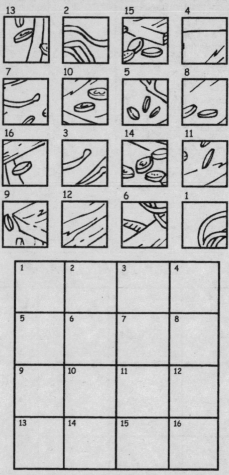

"SO HE MADE A WHIP OUT OF CORDS,
AND DROVE ALL FROM THE TEMPLE
AREA, BOTH *SHEEP* AND CATTLE; HE
SCATTERED THE COINS OF THE MONEY
CHANGERS AND OVERTURNED THEIR
TABLES."

JOHN 2:15

MISSING PIECES

Does the picture look a little unfinished to you? A lot of things are left out, but you can finish it by filling in as many missing pieces as you can find. Look carefully!

> "'I HAVE OTHER *SHEEP* THAT ARE NOT OF THIS SHEEP PEN. I MUST BRING THEM ALSO. THEY TOO WILL LISTEN TO MY VOICE, AND THERE SHALL BE ONE FLOCK AND ONE SHEPHERD.'"
>
> JOHN 10:16

COLOR THE PICTURE

"HE HAD THE *CAMELS* KNEEL DOWN NEAR THE WELL OUTSIDE THE TOWN; IT WAS TOWARD EVENING, THE TIME THE WOMEN GO OUT TO DRAW WATER."

GENESIS 24:11

WHAT'S DIFFERENT?

Look carefully at the pictures below. They look the same at first glance, but. . .are they? Circle any differences you find.

"HERDS OF *CAMELS* WILL COVER YOUR LAND, YOUNG CAMELS OF MIDIAN AND EPHAH. AND ALL FROM SHEBA WILL COME, BEARING GOLD AND INCENSE AND PROCLAIMING THE PRAISE OF THE LORD."

ISAIAH 60:6

COLOR THE PICTURE

"WHEN TWO FULL YEARS HAD PASSED, PHARAOH HAD A DREAM: HE WAS STANDING BY THE NILE, WHEN OUT OF THE RIVER THERE CAME UP SEVEN *COWS*, SLEEK AND FAT, AND THEY GRAZED AMONG THE REEDS. AFTER THEM, SEVEN OTHER COWS, UGLY AND GAUNT, CAME UP OUT OF THE NILE AND STOOD BESIDE THOSE ON THE RIVERBANK. AND THE COWS THAT WERE UGLY AND GAUNT ATE UP THE SEVEN SLEEK, FAT COWS. THEN PHARAOH WOKE UP."

GENESIS 41:1–4

COPY THE PICTURE

USING THE GRID, DRAW THE PICTURE BELOW.

COLOR THE PICTURE

"'YOU ARE A LION'S CUB, O JUDAH;
   YOU RETURN FROM THE PREY, MY SON.
LIKE A *LION* HE CROUCHES AND LIES
   DOWN,
   LIKE A LIONESS—WHO DARES TO
ROUSE HIM?'"

GENESIS 49:9

MiSSiNG PiECES

Does the picture look a little unfinished to you? A lot of things are left out, but you can finish it by filling in as many missing pieces as you can find. Look carefully!

"SAMSON WENT DOWN TO TIMNAH TOGETHER WITH HIS FATHER AND MOTHER. AS THEY APPROACHED THE VINEYARDS OF TIMNAH, SUDDENLY A YOUNG *LION* CAME ROARING TOWARD HIM. THE SPIRIT OF THE LORD CAME UPON HIM IN POWER SO THAT HE TORE THE LION APART WITH HIS BARE HANDS AS HE MIGHT HAVE TORN A YOUNG GOAT. BUT HE TOLD NEITHER HIS FATHER NOR HIS MOTHER WHAT HE HAD DONE."

JUDGES 14:5–6

PICTURE PIECES

PUT THE PICTURE PIECES IN THE RIGHT ORDER. DRAW WHAT IS IN EACH NUMBERED BOX BELOW INTO EACH BOX OF THE SAME NUMBER.

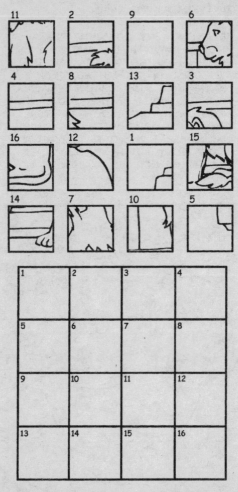

"THE THRONE HAD SIX STEPS, AND ITS BACK HAD A ROUNDED TOP. ON BOTH SIDES OF THE SEAT WERE ARMRESTS, WITH A *LION* STANDING BESIDE EACH OF THEM."

1 KINGS 10:19

WHAT'S DIFFERENT?

Look carefully at the pictures below. They look the same at first glance, but. . .are they? Circle any differences you find.

"'HE PROWLED AMONG THE *LIONS*, FOR
HE WAS NOW A STRONG LION.
HE LEARNED TO TEAR THE PREY
AND HE DEVOURED MEN.'"

EZEKIEL 19:6

HIDDEN LETTERS

Look carefully at the picture below. Then color in the areas that contain a square to reveal the hidden letters. Then use the letters to complete the verse below.

"BE SELF-CONTROLLED AND ALERT. YOUR ENEMY THE DEVIL PROWLS AROUND LIKE A ROARING __ __ __ __ LOOKING FOR SOMEONE TO DEVOUR."

1 PETER 5:8

__ __ __ __

MISSING PIECES

Does the picture look a little unfinished to you? A lot of things are left out, but you can finish it by filling in as many missing pieces as you can find. Look carefully!

"KEEP WATCH OVER YOURSELVES AND ALL THE FLOCK OF WHICH THE HOLY SPIRIT HAS MADE YOU OVERSEERS. BE SHEPHERDS OF THE CHURCH OF GOD, WHICH HE BOUGHT WITH HIS OWN BLOOD. I KNOW THAT AFTER I LEAVE, SAVAGE **WOLVES** WILL COME IN AMONG YOU AND WILL NOT SPARE THE FLOCK."

ACTS 20:28–29

PiCTURE PiECES

PUT THE PICTURE PIECES IN THE RIGHT ORDER.
DRAW WHAT IS IN EACH NUMBERED BOX
BELOW INTO EACH BOX OF THE SAME NUMBER.

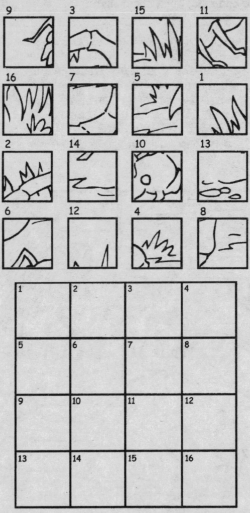

"AND THE AGONY THEY SUFFERED WAS
LIKE THAT OF THE STING OF A *SCORPION*
WHEN IT STRIKES A MAN."

REVELATION 9:5

COLOR THE PICTURE

"**ANTS** ARE CREATURES OF LITTLE STRENGTH, YET THEY STORE UP THEIR FOOD IN THE SUMMER."

PROVERBS 30:25

WHAT'S DIFFERENT?

Look carefully at the pictures below. They look the same at first glance, but. . .are they? Circle any differences you find.

"GO TO THE *ANT*, YOU SLUGGARD;
CONSIDER ITS WAYS AND BE WISE!"

PROVERBS 6:6

COLOR THE PICTURE

"IT IS GOD WHO ARMS ME WITH
   STRENGTH
   AND MAKES MY WAY PERFECT.
HE MAKES MY FEET LIKE THE FEET OF
   A *DEER*;
HE ENABLES ME TO STAND ON THE
   HEIGHTS."

PSALM 18:32–33

COPY THE PICTURE

USING THE GRID, DRAW THE PICTURE BELOW.

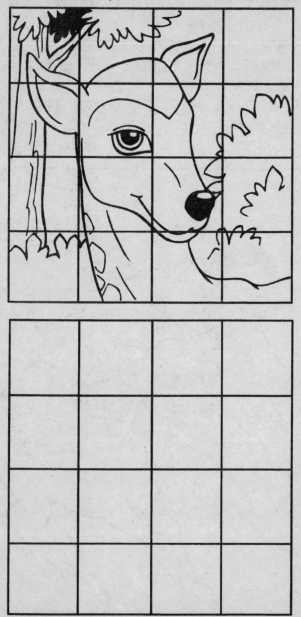

HIDDEN LETTERS

Color in the areas that contain a square to reveal the hidden letters. Then use the letters to complete the verse below.

"'BUT AMONG THE ISRAELITES NOT A
___ ___ ___ WILL BARK AT ANY MAN OR
ANIMAL.' THEN YOU WILL KNOW THAT
THE LORD MAKES A DISTINCTION
BETWEEN EGYPT AND ISRAEL."

EXODUS 11:7

___ ___ ___

PiCTURE PiECES

PUT THE PICTURE PIECES IN THE RIGHT ORDER.
DRAW WHAT IS IN EACH NUMBERED BOX
BELOW INTO EACH BOX OF THE SAME NUMBER.

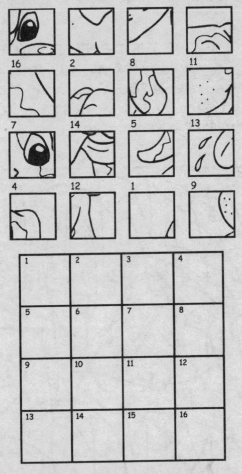

"SO GIDEON TOOK THE MEN DOWN TO
THE WATER. THERE THE LORD TOLD
HIM, 'SEPARATE THOSE WHO LAP THE
WATER WITH THEIR TONGUES LIKE A
DOG FROM THOSE WHO KNEEL DOWN
TO DRINK.'"

JUDGES 7:5

FiNiSH the PiCTURE

COMPLETE THE PICTURE BY DUPLICATING THE
FINISHED HALF ONTO THE UNFINISHED AREA.

"'I TELL YOU THE TRUTH,' JESUS
ANSWERED, 'THIS VERY NIGHT, BEFORE
THE *ROOSTER* CROWS, YOU WILL
DISOWN ME THREE TIMES.'"

MATTHEW 26:34

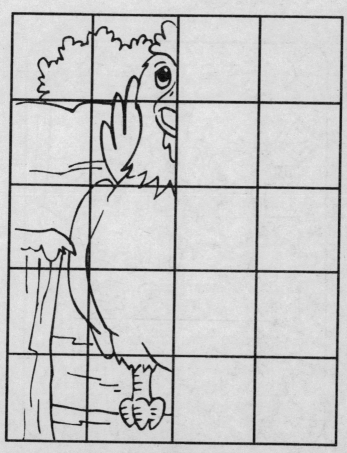

MISSING PIECES

Does the picture look a little unfinished to you? A lot of things are left out, but you can finish it by filling in as many missing pieces as you can find. Look carefully!

"ONE OF THE HIGH PRIEST'S SERVANTS, A RELATIVE OF THE MAN WHOSE EAR PETER HAD CUT OFF, CHALLENGED HIM, 'DIDN'T I SEE YOU WITH HIM IN THE OLIVE GROVE?' AGAIN PETER DENIED IT, AND AT THAT MOMENT A *ROOSTER* BEGAN TO CROW."

JOHN 18:26–27

COLOR THE PICTURE

"A *LIZARD* CAN BE CAUGHT WITH THE HAND,
  YET IT IS FOUND IN KINGS' PALACES."

PROVERBS 30:28

WHAT'S DIFFERENT?

Look carefully at the pictures below. They look the same at first glance, but. . .are they? Circle any differences you find.

"'THE GECKO, THE MONITOR LIZARD, THE WALL LIZARD, THE SKINK AND THE *CHAMELEON*.'"

LEVITICUS 11:30

HIDDEN LETTERS

Color in the areas that contain a square to reveal the hidden letters. Then use the letters to complete the verse below.

"THE LORD SAID, 'THROW IT ON THE GROUND.' MOSES THREW IT ON THE GROUND AND IT BECAME A ___ ___ ___ ___ ___, AND HE RAN FROM IT. THEN THE LORD SAID TO HIM, 'REACH OUT YOUR HAND AND TAKE IT BY THE TAIL.' SO MOSES REACHED OUT AND TOOK HOLD OF THE SNAKE AND IT TURNED BACK INTO A STAFF IN HIS HAND."

EXODUS 4:3–4

___ ___ ___ ___ ___

FiNiSH the PiCTURE

COMPLETE THE PICTURE BY DUPLICATING THE
FINISHED HALF ONTO THE UNFINISHED AREA.

"FOR HE WILL COMMAND HIS ANGELS
    CONCERNING YOU
    TO GUARD YOU IN ALL YOUR WAYS;
THEY WILL LIFT YOU UP IN THEIR
    HANDS,
SO THAT YOU WILL NOT STRIKE YOUR
    FOOT AGAINST A STONE.
YOU WILL TREAD UPON THE LION AND
    THE *COBRA*;
YOU WILL TRAMPLE THE GREAT LION
    AND THE SERPENT."

PSALM 91:11–13

PiCTURE PiECES

PUT THE PICTURE PIECES IN THE RIGHT ORDER.
DRAW WHAT IS IN EACH NUMBERED BOX
BELOW INTO EACH BOX OF THE SAME NUMBER.

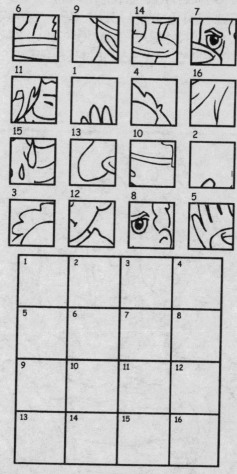

"DO NOT GAZE AT WINE WHEN IT
IS RED,
WHEN IT SPARKLES IN THE CUP,
WHEN IT GOES DOWN SMOOTHLY!
IN THE END IT BITES LIKE A *SNAKE*
AND POISONS LIKE A VIPER."

PROVERBS 23:31–32

COLOR THE PICTURE

"THEN ANOTHER SIGN APPEARED IN HEAVEN: AN ENORMOUS *RED DRAGON* WITH SEVEN HEADS AND TEN HORNS AND SEVEN CROWNS ON HIS HEADS."

REVELATION 12:3

WHAT'S DIFFERENT?

Look carefully at the pictures below. They look the same at first glance, but. . .are they? Circle any differences you find.

"THEN THE LORD SAID TO MOSES, 'TELL AARON, "STRETCH OUT YOUR HAND WITH YOUR STAFF OVER THE STREAMS AND CANALS AND PONDS, AND MAKE *FROGS* COME UP ON THE LAND OF EGYPT."'"

EXODUS 8:5

FiNiSH the PiCTURE

COMPLETE THE PICTURE BY DUPLICATING THE
FINISHED HALF ONTO THE UNFINISHED AREA.

"THE *OWL* WILL NEST THERE AND LAY
    EGGS,
    SHE WILL HATCH THEM, AND CARE
    FOR HER YOUNG UNDER THE
    SHADOW OF HER WINGS;
    THERE ALSO THE FALCONS WILL GATHER,
    EACH WITH ITS MATE."

ISAIAH 34:15

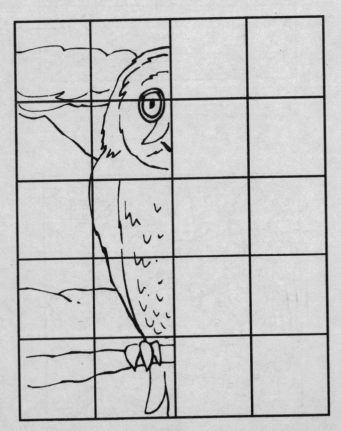

HIDDEN LETTERS

Look carefully at the pictures below. Then color in the areas that contain a square to reveal the hidden letters. Then use the letters to complete the verse below.

"BECAUSE OF MY LOUD GROANING
    I AM REDUCED TO SKIN AND BONES.
I AM LIKE A DESERT __ __ __,
    LIKE AN OWL AMONG THE RUINS.
I LIE AWAKE; I HAVE BECOME
    LIKE A BIRD ALONE ON A ROOF.
ALL DAY LONG MY ENEMIES TAUNT ME;
    THOSE WHO RAIL AGAINST ME USE
        MY NAME AS A CURSE."

PSALM 102:5–8

___ ___ ___

COLOR THE PICTURE

"'SO DESERT CREATURES AND *HYENAS*
WILL LIVE THERE,
AND THERE THE OWL WILL DWELL.
IT WILL NEVER AGAIN BE INHABITED
OR LIVED IN FROM GENERATION TO
GENERATION.'"

JEREMIAH 50:39

PICTURE PIECES

PUT THE PICTURE PIECES IN THE RIGHT ORDER.
DRAW WHAT IS IN EACH NUMBERED BOX
BELOW INTO EACH BOX OF THE SAME NUMBER.

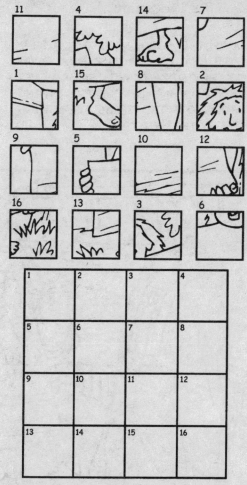

"BECAUSE OF THIS I WILL WEEP AND
      WAIL;
   I WILL GO ABOUT BAREFOOT AND
      NAKED.
I WILL HOWL LIKE A *JACKAL*
   AND MOAN LIKE AN OWL."

MICAH 1:8

MiSSiNG PieceS

Does the picture look a little unfinished to you? A lot of things are left out, but you can finish it by filling in as many missing pieces as you can find. Look carefully!

"AND THE LORD SAID TO MOSES, 'STRETCH OUT YOUR HAND OVER EGYPT SO THAT *LOCUSTS* WILL SWARM OVER THE LAND AND DEVOUR EVERYTHING GROWING IN THE FIELDS, EVERYTHING LEFT BY THE HAIL.'"

EXODUS 10:12

WHAT'S DIFFERENT?

Look carefully at the pictures below. They look the same at first glance, but. . .are they? Circle any differences you find.

"FOR I AM POOR AND NEEDY, AND MY HEART IS WOUNDED WITHIN ME. I FADE AWAY LIKE AN EVENING SHADOW; I AM SHAKEN OFF LIKE A *LOCUST.*"

PSALM 109:22–23

COPY THE PICTURE

USING THE GRID, DRAW THE PICTURE BELOW.

A BIG APPETITE FOR A LITTLE GUY

FiNiSH the PiCTURE

COMPLETE THE PICTURE BY DUPLICATING THE FINISHED HALF ONTO THE UNFINISHED AREA.

"OF THESE YOU MAY EAT ANY KIND OF LOCUST, KATYDID, *CRICKET* OR *GRASSHOPPER.* BUT ALL OTHER WINGED CREATURES THAT HAVE FOUR LEGS YOU ARE TO DETEST."

LEVITICUS 11:22–23

COLOR THE PICTURE

"ABRAHAM LOOKED UP AND THERE IN A THICKET HE SAW A *RAM* CAUGHT BY ITS HORNS. HE WENT OVER AND TOOK THE RAM AND SACRIFICED IT AS A BURNT OFFERING INSTEAD OF HIS SON. SO ABRAHAM CALLED THAT PLACE THE LORD WILL PROVIDE. AND TO THIS DAY IT IS SAID, 'ON THE MOUNTAIN OF THE LORD IT WILL BE PROVIDED.'"

GENESIS 22:13–14

PiCTURE PiECES

PUT THE PICTURE PIECES IN THE RIGHT ORDER.
DRAW WHAT IS IN EACH NUMBERED BOX
BELOW INTO EACH BOX OF THE SAME NUMBER.

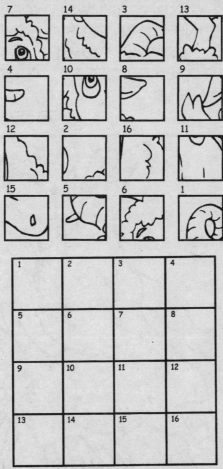

"I LOOKED UP, AND THERE BEFORE
ME WAS A *RAM* WITH TWO HORNS,
STANDING BESIDE THE CANAL, AND
THE HORNS WERE LONG. ONE OF THE
HORNS WAS LONGER THAN THE OTHER
BUT GREW UP LATER."

DANIEL 8:3

COLOR THE PICTURE

"AS I WATCHED, I HEARD AN *EAGLE* THAT WAS FLYING IN MIDAIR CALL OUT IN A LOUD VOICE: 'WOE! WOE! WOE TO THE INHABITANTS OF THE EARTH, BECAUSE OF THE TRUMPET BLASTS ABOUT TO BE SOUNDED BY THE OTHER THREE ANGELS!'"

REVELATION 8:13

HIDDEN LETTERS

Color in the areas that contain a square to reveal the hidden letters. Then use the letters to complete the verse below.

"CAST BUT A GLANCE AT RICHES, AND
    THEY ARE GONE,
FOR THEY WILL SURELY SPROUT
    WINGS
AND FLY OFF TO THE SKY LIKE AN

— — — — —."

PROVERBS 23:5

FiNiSH *the* PiCTURE

COMPLETE THE PICTURE BY DUPLICATING THE
FINISHED HALF ONTO THE UNFINISHED AREA.

"IN A DESERT LAND HE FOUND HIM,
    IN A BARREN AND HOWLING
        WASTE.
HE SHIELDED HIM AND CARED FOR HIM;
    HE GUARDED HIM AS THE APPLE OF
        HIS EYE,
LIKE AN *EAGLE* THAT STIRS UP ITS NEST
    AND HOVERS OVER ITS YOUNG,
THAT SPREADS ITS WINGS TO CATCH
        THEM
    AND CARRIES THEM ON ITS
        PINIONS."

DEUTERONOMY 32:10–11

MISSING PIECES

Does the picture look a little unfinished to you? A lot of things are left out, but you can finish it by filling in as many missing pieces as you can find. Look carefully!

"YOUR SONS HAVE FAINTED;
  THEY LIE AT THE HEAD OF EVERY
    STREET,
  LIKE *ANTELOPE* CAUGHT IN A NET.
THEY ARE FILLED WITH THE WRATH
    OF THE LORD
  AND THE REBUKE OF YOUR GOD."

ISAIAH 51:20

COPY THE PICTURE

USING THE GRID, DRAW THE PICTURE BELOW.

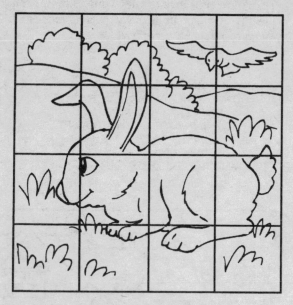

CUTE AS A BUNNY!

COLOR the PICTURE

"HUSHAI REPLIED TO ABSALOM, 'THE ADVICE AHITHOPHEL HAS GIVEN IS NOT GOOD THIS TIME. YOU KNOW YOUR FATHER AND HIS MEN; THEY ARE FIGHTERS, AND AS FIERCE AS A WILD *BEAR* ROBBED OF HER CUBS.'"

2 SAMUEL 17:7–8

WHAT'S DIFFERENT?

Look carefully at the pictures below. They look the same at first glance, but. . .are they? Circle any differences you find.

"BUT DAVID SAID TO SAUL, 'YOUR SERVANT HAS BEEN KEEPING HIS FATHER'S SHEEP. WHEN A LION OR A *BEAR* CAME AND CARRIED OFF A SHEEP FROM THE FLOCK, I WENT AFTER IT, STRUCK IT AND RESCUED THE SHEEP FROM ITS MOUTH.'"

1 SAMUEL 17:34–35

PiCTURE PiECES

PUT THE PICTURE PIECES IN THE RIGHT ORDER.
DRAW WHAT IS IN EACH NUMBERED BOX
BELOW INTO EACH BOX OF THE SAME NUMBER.

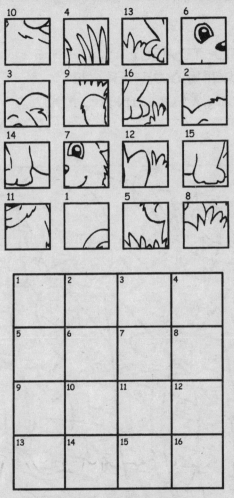

"'CAN YOU BRING FORTH THE
    CONSTELLATIONS IN THEIR SEASONS
OR LEAD OUT THE *BEAR* WITH ITS
    CUBS?'"

JOB 38:32

HIDDEN LETTERS

Color in the areas that contain a square to reveal the hidden letters. Then use the letters to complete the verse below.

"BETTER TO MEET A __ __ __ __
ROBBED OF HER CUBS
THAN A FOOL IN HIS FOLLY."

PROVERBS 17:12

__ __ __ __ __

COPY THE PICTURE

USING THE GRID, DRAW THE PICTURE BELOW.

IS "TEDDY" HIS NAME?

COLOR THE PICTURE

"IN THOSE DAYS I SAW MEN IN JUDAH TREADING WINEPRESSES ON THE SABBATH AND BRINGING IN GRAIN AND LOADING IT ON DONKEYS, TOGETHER WITH WINE, GRAPES, FIGS AND ALL OTHER KINDS OF LOADS. AND THEY WERE BRINGING ALL THIS INTO JERUSALEM ON THE SABBATH. THEREFORE I WARNED THEM AGAINST SELLING FOOD ON THAT DAY. MEN FROM TYRE WHO LIVED IN JERUSALEM WERE BRINGING IN *FISH* AND ALL KINDS OF MERCHANDISE AND SELLING THEM IN JERUSALEM ON THE SABBATH TO THE PEOPLE OF JUDAH."

NEHEMIAH 13:15–16

MISSING PIECES

Does the picture look a little unfinished to you? A lot of things are left out, but you can finish it by filling in as many missing pieces as you can find. Look carefully!

"THEN GOD SAID, 'LET US MAKE MAN IN OUR IMAGE, IN OUR LIKENESS, AND LET THEM RULE OVER THE *FISH* OF THE SEA AND THE BIRDS OF THE AIR, OVER THE LIVESTOCK, OVER ALL THE EARTH, AND OVER ALL THE CREATURES THAT MOVE ALONG THE GROUND.'"

GENESIS 1:26

WHAT'S DIFFERENT?

Look carefully at the pictures below. They look the same at first glance, but. . .are they? Circle any differences you find.

"'ONCE AGAIN, THE KINGDOM OF HEAVEN IS LIKE A NET THAT WAS LET DOWN INTO THE LAKE AND CAUGHT ALL KINDS OF *FISH*.'"

MATTHEW 13:47

Finish the Picture

COMPLETE THE PICTURE BY DUPLICATING THE FINISHED HALF ONTO THE UNFINISHED AREA.

"TAKING THE FIVE LOAVES AND THE TWO *FISH* AND LOOKING UP TO HEAVEN, HE GAVE THANKS AND BROKE THEM. THEN HE GAVE THEM TO THE DISCIPLES TO SET BEFORE THE PEOPLE. THEY ALL ATE AND WERE SATISFIED, AND THE DISCIPLES PICKED UP TWELVE BASKETFULS OF BROKEN PIECES THAT WERE LEFT OVER."

LUKE 9:16–17

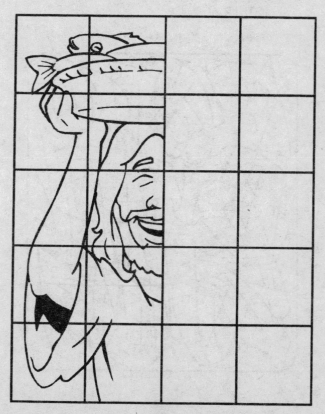

HIDDEN LETTERS

Look carefully at the pictures below. Then color in the areas that contain a square to reveal the hidden letters. Then use the letters to complete the verse below.

"WHEN YOU SOW, YOU DO NOT PLANT THE BODY THAT WILL BE, BUT JUST A SEED, PERHAPS OF WHEAT OR OF SOMETHING ELSE. BUT GOD GIVES IT A BODY AS HE HAS DETERMINED, AND TO EACH KIND OF SEED HE GIVES ITS OWN BODY. ALL FLESH IS NOT THE SAME: MEN HAVE ONE KIND OF FLESH, ANIMALS HAVE ANOTHER, BIRDS ANOTHER AND __ __ __ __ ANOTHER."

1 CORINTHIANS 15:37–39

___ ___ ___ ___

196

MISSING PIECES

Does the picture look a little unfinished to you? A lot of things are left out, but you can finish it by filling in as many missing pieces as you can find. Look carefully!

"'A WICKED AND ADULTEROUS GENERATION ASKS FOR A MIRACULOUS SIGN! BUT NONE WILL BE GIVEN IT EXCEPT THE SIGN OF THE PROPHET JONAH. FOR AS JONAH WAS THREE DAYS AND THREE NIGHTS IN THE BELLY OF A HUGE *FISH*, SO THE SON OF MAN WILL BE THREE DAYS AND THREE NIGHTS IN THE HEART OF THE EARTH.'"

MATTHEW 12:39–40

Finish the Picture

COMPLETE THE PICTURE BY DUPLICATING THE FINISHED HALF ONTO THE UNFINISHED AREA.

"BUT THE LORD PROVIDED A GREAT *FISH* TO SWALLOW JONAH, AND JONAH WAS INSIDE THE FISH THREE DAYS AND THREE NIGHTS."

JONAH 1:17

COPY THE PICTURE

USING THE GRID, DRAW THE PICTURE BELOW.

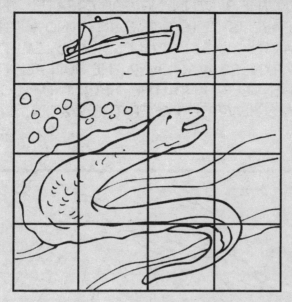

LEVIATHAN...OR SOMETHING ELSE?

COLOR THE PICTURE

"IN THE BEGINNING GOD CREATED THE HEAVENS AND THE EARTH. NOW THE EARTH WAS FORMLESS AND EMPTY, DARKNESS WAS OVER THE SURFACE OF THE DEEP, AND THE SPIRIT OF GOD WAS HOVERING OVER THE WATERS."

GENESIS 1:1–2

HIDDEN LETTERS

Look carefully at the pictures below. Then color in the areas that contain a square to reveal the hidden letters. Then use the letters to complete the verse below.

"SO GOD CREATED THE GREAT CREATURES OF THE SEA AND EVERY LIVING AND MOVING THING WITH WHICH THE WATER TEEMS, ACCORDING TO THEIR KINDS, AND EVERY WINGED _ _ _ _ ACCORDING TO ITS KIND. AND GOD SAW THAT IT WAS GOOD. GOD BLESSED THEM AND SAID, 'BE FRUITFUL AND INCREASE IN NUMBER AND FILL THE WATER IN THE SEAS, AND LET THE BIRDS INCREASE ON THE EARTH.'"

GENESIS 1:21–22

_ _ _ _ _

MISSING PIECES

Does the picture look a little unfinished to you? A lot of things are left out, but you can finish it by filling in as many missing pieces as you can find. Look carefully!

"AND GOD SAID, 'LET THE LAND PRODUCE LIVING CREATURES ACCORDING TO THEIR KINDS: LIVESTOCK, CREATURES THAT MOVE ALONG THE GROUND, AND WILD ANIMALS, EACH ACCORDING TO ITS KIND.' AND IT WAS SO. GOD MADE THE WILD ANIMALS ACCORDING TO THEIR KINDS, THE LIVESTOCK ACCORDING TO THEIR KINDS, AND ALL THE CREATURES THAT MOVE ALONG THE GROUND ACCORDING TO THEIR KINDS. AND GOD SAW THAT IT WAS GOOD."

GENESIS 1:24–25

COPY THE PICTURE

USING THE GRID, DRAW THE PICTURE BELOW.

A BIG ONE!

COLOR THE PICTURE

"THEN GOD SAID, 'I GIVE YOU EVERY
SEED-BEARING PLANT ON THE FACE OF
THE WHOLE EARTH AND EVERY TREE
THAT HAS FRUIT WITH SEED IN IT.
THEY WILL BE YOURS FOR FOOD. AND
TO ALL THE BEASTS OF THE EARTH AND
ALL THE BIRDS OF THE AIR AND ALL
THE CREATURES THAT MOVE ON THE
GROUND—EVERYTHING THAT HAS THE
BREATH OF LIFE IN IT—I GIVE EVERY
GREEN PLANT FOR FOOD.' AND IT WAS
SO. GOD SAW ALL THAT HE HAD MADE,
AND IT WAS VERY GOOD. AND THERE
WAS EVENING, AND THERE WAS
MORNING—THE SIXTH DAY."

GENESIS 1:29–31

≡ANSWER PAGES≡

Page 71

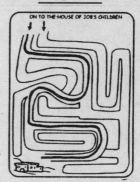

ON TO THE HOUSE OF JOB'S CHILDREN

Page 72

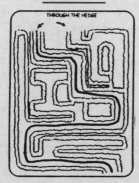

ROAMING THROUGH THE EARTH

F O R T H

Page 73

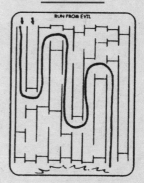

RUN FROM EVIL

Page 74

THROUGH THE HEDGE

Page 75

OUT FROM GOD'S PRESENCE

Page 76

Page 77

B U R N E D

Page 78

Page 79

Page 80

W O R S H I P

Page 81

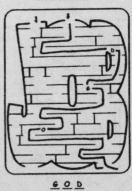

G O D

206

Page 82

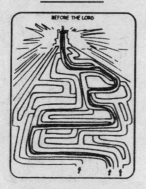

Page 83

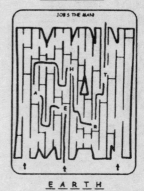

E A R T H

Page 84

S T R E T C H

Page 85

Page 86

F O O L I S H

Page 87

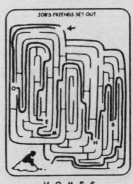

H O M E S

Page 88

GOING THROUGH FEAR

P E A C E

Page 89

FEEBLE HANDS

Page 90

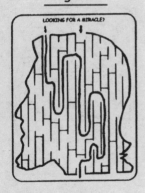

LOOKING FOR A MIRACLE?

Page 91

A N G U I S H

Page 92

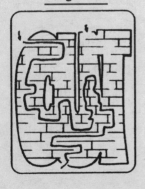

Page 93

TRYING TO FIND HOPE

S T R E N G T H

Page 94

Page 95

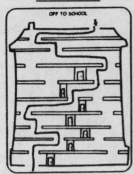

Page 96

T E S T

Page 97

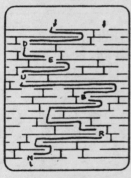

B U R D E N

Page 98

F O R G I V E

Page 99

Page 100

A L M I G H T Y

Page 101

M O U T H

Page 102

Page 103

Z O P H A R

Page 104

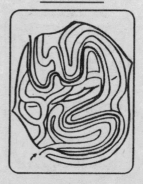

Page 105

Page 106

A R G U E

Page 107

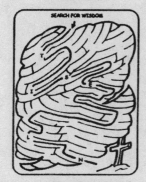

S I L E N T

Page 108

Page 109

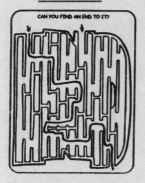

Page 110

S H A K E

Page 111

Page 112

Page 113

Page 114

Page 115

A D M I T

Page 116

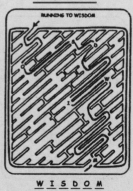

W I S D O M

Page 117

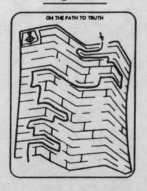

Page 118

LOOKING FOR ANSWERS

F A M I L Y

Page 119

NOTHING MORE TO SAY

Page 120

Page 121

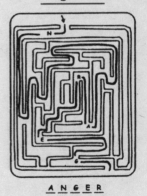

A N G E R

Page 122

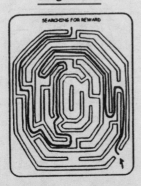

SEARCHING FOR REWARD

Page 123

EMPTY TALK

Page 124

C O U N S E L

Page 125

WHERE IS THE EARTH'S FOUNDATION?

Page 126

WOULD YOU CORRECT HIM?

C O R R E C T

Page 127

SPEAK ONLY ONCE

Page 128

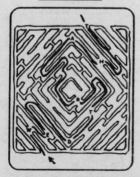

T H W A R T E D

Page 130

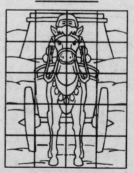

214

Page 132

Page 133

Page 134

Page 135

H O R S E S

Page 138

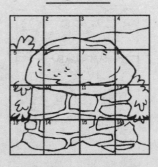

Page 139

Page 140

Page 141

Page 142

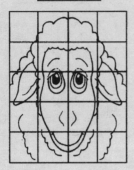

S H E E P

Page 144

Page 145

Page 147

Page 151

Page 152

Page 153

Page 154

L I O N

Page 155

Page 156

Page 158

Page 161

D O G

Page 162

Page 163

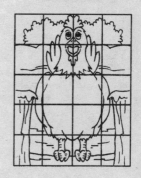

Page 164

Page 166

Page 167

S N A K E

Page 168

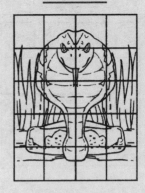

Page 169

Page 171

Page 172

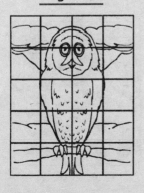

Page 173

O W L

Page 175

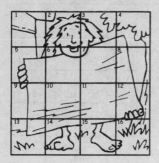

Page 176

Page 177

Page 179

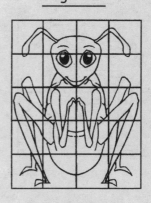

Page 181

Page 183

E A G L E

Page 184

Page 185

Page 188

Page 189

Page 190

Page 193

Page 194

Page 195

Page 196

F I S H

Page 197

Page 198

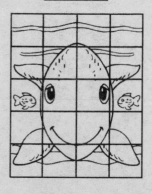

Page 201

B I R D

Check out these other

KIDS' BIBLE ACTIVITY BOOKS

from

Barbour Publishing

ISBN 978-1-60260-863-4

ISBN 978-1-60260-862-7

ISBN 978-1-60260-861-0

- 224 pages of fun
- Perfect for rainy days, car trips, and Sunday school classes

Available wherever books are sold.